Longing to Belong

Filling the Longings of our Hearts with the
Hope of Home

Ellen Chauvin

Soaked & Sprouting Ministries

What others are saying about Longing to Belong:

Ellen's wisdom, honesty, and endearing humor create a space for even the deepest longings of our hearts. For anyone feeling untethered by grief, *Longing to Belong* is your road map home.

~Mary Kathryn Tiller, co-author of *New Mercies: A Devotional Set for Moms*, speaker, and co-host of **Writing Off Social: The Podcast**

Ellen Chauvin does a masterful job of helping her readers pinpoint the unsettled feeling many of us have — a longing to belong in a world where we feel like misfits. Ellen skillfully weaves her personal story of grief alongside the stories of biblical characters who navigated grief and difficult situations. She made me smile as she recounted her struggle with her name and brought me to tears as I thought of the joy my mom must have living with Jesus. Read this book. It will change your view of heaven and give you a better understanding of where our home truly is.

~Carmen Horne, author of *Out of Words* and *Grace Maps*, **Your Hope Coach** podcast host, and board certified Life Coach

"Heaven's sounding sweeter all the time," I remember my precious mother-in-law singing the words of that old hymn as if they were the cry of her heart. The more time I spend on this earth, the more I relate to that deep longing. I want to know more about heaven and what awaits us there. In *Longing to Belong*, Ellen Chauvin takes us on a journey to learn about our connection to our true home. With personal experiences and deep biblical insight, Ellen offers hope for our questions about heaven and shows us what our heavenly home means for our lives today. *Longing to Belong* is a must-read about the sweetness of heaven!

~Kristine Brown, author of **Over It** and **Cinched**, teacher, host of **Kristine Brown** YouTube channel

Longing to Belong addresses a question all of us have asked but don't often express: Where do I belong? Like a trusted friend, Chauvin answers this question with relatable stories, deep scriptural insights, and a healthy dose of humor. She tenderly points her readers to the One who *is* our home and gives practical tools to ground her on the journey. This book will encourage anyone who has ever felt like a wanderer in a strange land, longing for a place to call home.

~Abby McDonald, author of **Shift**, writing coach, and contributor of Proverbs 31 Ministries

It's been said that we have a God-sized hole in our hearts that is longing to be filled. We desire to belong to something bigger than ourselves and until we learn how to fill that hole with a relationship with Jesus, we will forever be searching. In **Longing to Belong**, author Ellen Chauvin takes her readers on a journey through both grief and wholeness as she weaves Biblical truths in and out at every turn. You will laugh, you will cry, and you will find your ultimate belonging right where Jesus is.

~April Rodgers, author of **Made to Shine** and **Resting in Jesus**, owner of Reflecting Light Ministries at aprilrodgers.com

Ellen's vulnerability about loss, death, and longing strikes a chord in my heart that is relatable and hopeful. She eloquently shares that what we don't know can shape our eternal perspective if we're not careful. But **Longing to Belong** is a beautiful reminder that embracing the hope of no more tears, death, or longing must encourage all exiles not to give up! God created us for eternity with Him, and it will be so good that it's beyond what we can imagine!

~Melanie Davis Porter, Author, Writer and Speaker

In a world full of messages that make us question where we really belong, I'm so grateful that Ellen answered God's call to write this book. We must fill ourselves with truth to help not only ourselves but the next generation of seekers. I'm empowered by Ellen's reminder that "waiting for Christ's return shouldn't be passive." The way she guides us through these pages to set our hearts and daily steps focused on getting closer to Jesus encourages us to help others do the same.

~Kim Stewart, marketing strategist, host of **Book Marketing Mania** podcast

Easy to read and relate to, **Longing to Belong** is a practical guide to navigating those spaces of uncertainty and doubt as we journey through life. We do not always understand the paths we have to travel, but we can learn from the experiences of those who have traveled those paths before us. This book is a good resource for those in those dark spaces of uncertainty, doubt, and a longing to reach a place you can call home.

~Boma Somiari, editor of *The Message* magazine

Longing to Belong takes us on a journey to fill the yearning of our hearts with the promise of our eternal home. Ellen Chauvin has written a must-read guide for anyone who is longing to belong and wonders if this is all there is to life.

~Stephanie K. Adams, Author of *In the Shadow of the Cross: Following Jesus Through His Last Days*

ISBN: 979-8-218-51533-1

Cover Design: Hannah Linder Designs

Editing Services: Liz Giertz

Author Photo: John Chauvin

This book is dedicated:

To my husband John.
Thank you for your prayers, patience, and encouragement.
I love you.

And to the memory of my sweet Mama, who is sitting with Jesus,
waiting for the day all things are made new. Mama, we'll be home
soon. Save a place for us.

CONTENTS

INTRODUCTION

My friend examined the family portrait hanging prominently on the wall. The picture her mom was excited for her to see. She looked and saw her parents and all her brothers.

"The one thing missing," she told me, "was me! They didn't include me in the family portrait."

All she wanted was to be included. She longed to belong.

Filling the Longings

Haven't we all felt this way? Aren't we all searching for the place where we belong and the people we belong to? Belonging gives us a sense of purpose.

Are you looking for things to fill you? A great job, more money. Maybe you'll feel complete when you have your dream marriage and the home to go with it. Consider this: the more you search, the emptier you will feel.

This is a road I have traveled. Trying to take my mind off the void in my heart, I resorted to mindless social media scrolling. I sensed there should be more. I just couldn't grasp what it was. So I ended up watching countless uninspired and dull television series to numb the feeling of loss.

Shouldn't there be more to this life? Shouldn't all the good things we've accomplished and accumulated prove that we belong? Why then, do we still seek to fill the void in our souls? These are the questions I've asked myself. Maybe you have, too.

But what if this great chasm in our hearts is a deep spiritual longing? What if our problem is the beginning of our solution? What if we realize we don't belong?

Longing for Home

How can that be? How can we not belong? God created the earth and populated it with man. We belong here, don't we?

For now, yes. But ultimately we belong with Jesus, who is in Heaven. Our time on earth is a pilgrimage toward our true home with Him.

What if we embrace the fact that we are strangers and exiles here, and recognize the life we live is a journey toward our forever home? It is how we traverse this journey that matters.

For instance, some people meander through life. They wander aimlessly without a clear destination. As followers of Jesus, there are times we meander, walking in circles and never making progress.

Most Christ followers coddiwomple through life. *What?* Coddiwomple. Surely you've seen it in a meme on social media. That's how I encountered it. It's a brilliant word that means to travel purposefully toward a vague destination.

If we're honest, most of us live like this. We wander around, heading toward this mysterious place we call home, but do not know where it is, what it is, or what we'll do when we get there. We don't know what to do in the waiting. Every day we continue to coddiwomple around, trying to fill the longings in our hearts. Most of us fail to realize that what we long for is our ultimate home, the home we cannot reach while tethered to this life.

It's a Journey

Longing to Belong is a journey to fill the longings of our hearts with the hope of home. And this home we are hoping for is not a vague destination. It's an actual place where we will live forever. We don't have to wait until we get there to know more about our eternal home.

Longing to Belong helps us understand God has better things planned for us. We will discover why we need to learn about Heaven, how to focus on eternity, and why we should rejoice as strangers and exiles in this world.

They (whoever "they" are) say every journey has a story. My Mama's death was the beginning of my journey. This book is my story of finding home and the truth that got me there.

Perhaps you've been longing for home, for more, for better. If so, this book is for you.

Longing to Belong is not a prescriptive work. It is a field guide for the path ahead. Written in three parts, it will guide you along the way.

Part 1—Realize We Don't Belong, addresses several common longings of our hearts. Rather than settle for the fulfillment of these trivial and fleeting longings, Part 1 describes the "better" God has prepared for each of us.

Part 2—Recognize Heaven is Home, answers questions we have about Heaven. Why learn about it? Why is it home? When we learn about our eternal destination, we won't coddiwomple through life.

It will no longer be a vague destination. We know exactly where we are going, and we will look forward to it.

Part 3—Rejoice as an Exile, is a guide to direct us along the way. It gives practical advice on how to live as an exile while we wait for home. Waiting can be hard, especially if we only have a fuzzy idea of what we are waiting for. When we learn about and come to know Heaven, we can wait with faith, confidence, and a longing for home.

When we finish this journey, we will be different. It's my prayer that we will have an eternal mindset. We will long for and look forward to Heaven.

So, keep your bags packed, enjoy the journey, and let Revelation 22:20 be your prayer: "Come, Lord Jesus!"

Part 1

· · · · · · ● · · · · · ·

On Our Journey Home

We

Realize We Don't Belong

Chapter 1

LONGING TO BELONG

The fact that our heart yearns for something earth can't supply is proof that Heaven must be our home. ~C.S. Lewis

I WOKE WITH A gasp, confused and dazed, sleep clouding my eyes and memory. What day is it? Where am I?

Throwing on a robe, I walked into the living room. It was silent, save for the tick, tick, tick of the clock. It sounded like a time bomb about to explode, destroying everything. But it is my heart that is shattered.

Glancing around, things seemed odd. Like I haven't lived in my home for several months.

In fact, I have not. Two months ago, I began the hardest journey of my life. My mom suffered a stroke. All of a sudden, I was packing "go" bags and traveling back and forth between Mississippi (where Mama was) and my home in Louisiana. All while trying not to get behind at work and keep some semblance of normalcy in our home.

Almost two months to the day Mama had her stroke, she passed away. Oh, how my heart hurt. Now, here I am, feeling like an intruder in my own house. How is it possible to live in a house over a decade and not feel at home?

I took a second look. Things seemed different. Like someone had rearranged the furniture. Familiar, but not quite right. Nothing felt the same. I was a stranger here.

When the doctors sent Mama home on hospice care, I wanted to spend as much time in Mississippi as possible. To be with her, to be with my family, so we could gather around and love on her. Mama always said, "I just don't want to die alone." Oh, sweet Mama. We will not let that happen!

Slow tears trickled down my face at her funeral. I watched the pallbearers carry Mama ever so gently up the steps into the white clapboard church she called home. The sweltering July day would have been unbearable if I had noticed. I did not. There was a fog clouding my senses. The only thing that could get me through the next few hours was the grace of God.

Trudging down the aisle, it was difficult to put one foot in front of the other. It felt like I was walking through a river of mud. Struggling. But there were things to do. People and family to greet. Slowly they arrived, their murmured condolences not even beginning to comfort my grieving heart.

Her service was beautiful! Exactly what she would have wanted. Mama's pastor told us of her love for Jesus and laid out the plan of salvation. Her church family fed us after the funeral, hugging and loving on us.

"We loved Miss Ann. She was a sweetheart, and so kind! We will surely miss her." Oh, how well I knew!

One bittersweet scene replays in my mind. On a whiteboard in the church choir room, these words:

Ann Eason

July 28, 2011

Oh happy day!

Oh...happy...day. I was trying, but my heart shattered like broken glass. It's a hard thing to lose a mama. She was the glue that held our family together. What now?

I knew I should rejoice for my mom. She is healed, whole, and home. God's Word says that I shouldn't grieve as those who have no hope. But I wasn't thinking of any kind of hope right now. Just that Mama was gone, and I missed her.

Eventually, I headed back home to Louisiana. But I left my heart in Mississippi. It amazed me how quickly I had reverted to being a southern belle from Mississippi, rather than a sweet and salty gal from south Louisiana. Memories from Mama's stay in the hospital flooded my thoughts.

One day, a nurse came into Mama's hospital room.

"Hey there! The docs wanna do a little procedure on your mom. It's called a *ThisisnotsomethingIknowanythingabout*. Nothin' major. It should help keep th' feedin' tube in. I need you to sign right here with your approval." (I couldn't pronounce nor spell the procedure she was telling me about.)

Honestly, I didn't understand some of her "Mississippi speak." But I nodded my head.

"Yes, of course!"

At once, I realized my error: I did not know what medical treatment the nurse was talking about! And I agreed to it! I heard the nurse's words but didn't actually understand. "Crawfishing" my approval, I had to backtrack (because crawfish swim backward) and say "no."

"I'm sorry. I'm not the one who can approve medical treatments. Let me get my brother and sister-in-law!" I wanted to add this: *They live here in Mississippi and will understand everything you say!*

Good times in Mississippi, even though they were hard. I missed being there. My siblings were there. We bonded again, and the family bond is hard to break. We discussed all the good and fun times, as well as our mom's medical care, her finances, and all the hard conversations.

"Y'all, I found this paper Mama gave me a year or so ago. We need to discuss it."

The paper, written in my mom's handwriting, was a list of everything she wanted at her funeral. She had the hymns and who would sing them. She listed each pallbearer by name. And then it came to the clothes she wanted to be buried in. Her list said, "The children know which dress."

Looking at my brothers and sisters-in-law, I asked,

"Any ideas?"

Blank stares.

"I don't, do you?"

"Nope, not at all."

Our final decision was her yellow pinstripe pants set with a matching top. She loved that outfit!

We spent quality time with each other, connecting on a deeper level than the usual weekend visits provided. We laughed and told stories about Mama. I reconnected with my Mississippi family, and without realizing it I disconnected from all the family happenings in Louisiana.

Mississippi is home. It's where I grew up. For the first time in thirty years, I felt like a stranger in Louisiana. For the last two months, I lived with a foot in each world. Mississippi. Louisiana. I didn't feel like I belonged here. Or there. I was homesick. For Mama. For the family time we had shared. For home, wherever that may be. Grief washed over me. I was an outsider. A foreigner. I wanted to belong. Somewhere. Be a part of something.

I was a stranger in a strange land.

Like Abraham.

Abraham the Stranger

"Sarah, oh Sarah, how I will miss you!" Tears streamed down Abraham's face. Wailing in lament for his beautiful wife, Abraham tore his cloak in grief.

It was in Hebron that Sarah breathed her last breath. Abraham grieved her loss and mourned for her. After a time, Abraham knew he needed to care for Sarah in death, as in life. He had to purchase a burial plot.

"I am a stranger and a sojourner among you; give me a burial site among you that I may bury my dead out of my sight" (Genesis 23:4).

Abraham approached the sons of Heth to purchase land for Sarah's entombment. By this time, he and Sarah had been living in the Promised Land for over sixty years. Why didn't he own land?

The sons of Heth, who owned the land Abraham needed, had great respect for him: "Hear us, my lord, you are a mighty prince among us" (Genesis 23:6).

My lord.

Mighty prince.

With such respect shown, they must have known Abraham. They knew the type of man he was. Abraham was no stranger to them.

Why, then, did Abraham call himself a stranger and sojourner?

Grief can do this. It can make you feel like a stranger. When you are grieving, you feel all alone. No one knows what you are going through.

Just as my grief separated me from my Louisiana family, making me feel alone and like I didn't belong, Abraham's grief could have done the same. He and Sarah had lived many years together. In biblical times, a young woman would have married in her early teens. It's safe to say that Sarah and Abraham had been married for over 100 years. That's a long time to live with someone! What would he do now without his partner by his side? Abraham felt the loss of his beautiful Sarah acutely.

They had many adventures together beginning over sixty years ago when God called them to become nomads.

Abraham the Faithful Servant

God invited Abraham to become an exile from his homeland in Ur.

From there, God called Abram (as he was known then) to move away from his home, his people, and the gods he knew. Abe (That's what I like to call him; I love nicknames, especially short ones!), lived in Haran with his father, Terah (Genesis 12). He was seventy-five years old when God called him to move away. Seventy-five!! And do you know what Abe did? He left. He departed from his home. No questions asked.

Was Abram tempted to leave because of God's promises? According to His promise, God was to make Abram into a great nation and make Abram's name great. He also promised to bless Abram. Abram may have been looking for a better life, and God's plan sounded like just the ticket. But I don't think so.

Abram left his home in faith, not knowing where God was taking him (Hebrews 11:8). He walked by faith, not by sight. Abram's faith earned him righteousness.

To be honest, I'm not sure my faith would be that strong. Well, maybe my faith would hold up, but my curiosity would break down and get the best of me.

"Where are we going? When will we get there? WHY?"

But not Abe. He obeyed. In faith, Abram left his home.

Abram, Sarai, his nephew Lot, and all their possessions set out for the land of Canaan. It was here the Lord appeared to Abram and said, "I'll give all this land to your descendants." Now, Abram knew exactly where God was leading him.

Abram pitched his tent in Bethel and built an altar. There, he called on the name of the Lord. This God, who took him out of Ur of the Chaldeans, out of a land of "little g" gods, was worthy of his worship. This God was worth trusting and getting to know.

Unfortunately, there was a famine in the land. Abe and Sarai had to leave. They went to Egypt in search of food. When they arrived, Abe asked something of Sarai. Something very odd.

I imagine Abe's conversation with his wife could have gone something like this:

"Sarai, babe, could you pretend to be my sister? You are so beautiful! The Egyptians will say, 'That gorgeous woman is his wife! Let's kill him and take her.' If you pretend to be my sister, they will spare my life."

Hmmm, where was Abram's faith now? He was devising a plan to preserve his own life for God's promise of many descendants, as if the Creator of the universe needed any help keeping him alive. Abe's actions implied he didn't completely trust God when He said, "I will make you a great nation." After all, a great nation takes people, children Abe wouldn't have unless he lived. So he did what many of us do; he took circumstances into his own hands instead of waiting on the Lord.

God, in His infinite love and grace, delivered Abe and Sarai out of Egypt unharmed. Not only that, He reaffirmed His promise to Abram of a son. Abe assumed one of his servants would be the heir since he and Sarai had no children. But no! God assured Abe this son would come from his own loins.

By this time, Abram and Sarai had lived in Canaan for ten years. Now, it was Sarai who grew impatient waiting on the Lord. She decided to give God's promise a helping hand. Sarai and Abe believed in God and His promises, but not enough to wait on Him. Sarai gave her maidservant Hagar to Abram, hoping Hagar would bear his child. Sure enough Abram and Hagar's son Ishmael was born.

But God! His plans are better. He told Abe that his son would come from Sarah (the new name God gave Sarai), his wife. "I will bless her and give you a son from her...Kings of nations will be among her descendants" (Genesis 17:16 NLT).

At this, Abraham laughed to himself. I can't say I blame him, since he was already 99 years old and Sarah was 89. They were WAY too old to have babies, even back in those days. Many commentaries say Abraham laughed in disbelief. However, one commentator sees it this way: Abraham laughed in joyful belief.[2] He tells us "joy was uppermost in Abraham's heart."

"A child? With Sarah? At long last, we will have a child!" Abraham knew God would keep His word and bless him and Sarah with a son. A year later, Isaac was born to them!

The longer Abraham walked with the Lord, the stronger his faith grew.

The longer Abraham walked with the Lord, the stronger his faith grew. And the more obedient he became.

But what would Abe do when God asked the impossible of him?

When Isaac was older, God told Abraham to do something no parent in their right mind would agree to. He asked Abraham to sacrifice his one and only son, Isaac (Genesis 22:2). Abraham's response was staggering; he obeyed, instantly and without question.

Abe shuffled up to Mount Moriah dragging his heavy heart as he led Isaac up the mountain. He knew he was supposed to kill his precious son. I can only imagine what went through Abraham's mind as he watched his son carry the wood for his own sacrifice.

Lord, I love You; I believe your promises. But this? How can I possibly sacrifice Isaac? My only son. The son that will bring forth many descendants to make a great nation for You! And now You want me to kill him? Oh, Lord, this is too much! How can I? I don't understand, but I trust You.

The author of Hebrews gives us a glimpse of what Abraham was thinking (Hebrews 11:17-19). Abraham believed God would raise Isaac from the dead. That is the earth-shattering faith of Abraham. He trusted in God's promises of descendants and nations so much that he would sacrifice Isaac. He knew God would make it right somehow, someway. And God did. He provided a ram for the sacrifice, saving Isaac.

Abraham the Wandering Nomad

Through the ups and downs and many adventures, Abraham had Sarah by his side. And now, all these years later, she was gone. Abraham was alone and felt like a stranger in a strange land. Grief does that to you. But then again, so will living like a nomad.

Abraham and Sarah led a nomadic life, living in tents. Because he had cattle and herds, Abe had to move with the flocks to keep them fed and watered. But he never seemed to settle down.

From Haran, Abraham went to Shechem. From Shechem, he went to Bethel and Ai. The famine led Abraham to Egypt. On each leg of his journey, Abe packed up his tents, his wife, his family, his servant, and his livestock and headed out. It was not travel like we are used to today. It was hard and wearisome.

After Egypt, Abe headed back to Bethel. It was here that he and his nephew Lot separated. The land could not support both of them, with their livestock and families. And there had been quarrels among their herdsmen. Abraham let Lot choose his portion of the land, and Abe took whatever was left. Lot chose the valley of the Jordan and Abraham settled in the land of Canaan. There, Abraham moved his tents to Hebron, at the oaks of Mamre.

Sarah's death at this location left Abe in a difficult situation. He didn't own any land. Not even a parcel to bury his beloved wife.

It's hard to imagine, isn't it? Wandering around in a land given to you by God, and yet never owning property to call home; living in tents and never building a house to live in. It was all so...temporary. Abraham needed to purchase land to bury Sarah.

Perhaps this was why Abe called himself a sojourner.

Despite being well respected in the area, Abraham still feels like a stranger and sojourner. Though he is called "my lord" and "mighty prince" (Genesis 23:6) he still feels like an outsider. Perhaps it was grief at Sarah's death or maybe his nomadic lifestyle, but Abe didn't feel at home.

What was Abraham talking about? What did it mean to him to be a stranger?

In the original Hebrew, a stranger is defined as "anyone who is not native to a given land or among a given people. Strangers or aliens were those living in a strange land among strange people. Their stay was temporary, or they did not identify with the group among whom they were living, no matter how long they stayed."[3]

Abraham was a stranger because he was not native to the land. The Hittites, Perrizites, and Canaanites still lived there. Abraham had strangers all around him but never had a home. He wasn't living with his people. Ah, how well I knew the feeling in the aftermath of my mother's death. You act differently. You talk differently (or maybe they act and talk differently!). And you don't fit in. So, you keep moving. You become a sojourner, or a foreigner.

According to *The Complete Word Study Dictionary*, "This word (sojourner) implies temporary visitors who were dependent in some way on the nation in which they were residing. It denotes a wanderer with close ties to the land occupied by another people (Genesis 23:4). Temporary resident."[4] A stranger in a strange land. A temporary resident. That is what he called himself. But wasn't Abraham exactly where he was supposed to be?

Yes and no.

Yes, Abraham was in the Promised Land and was now a landowner in Canaan. But he never belonged there. He knew there was more. In life, Abraham and his family were strangers and sojourners. Temporary residents, not belonging here or there. In death, they were heirs of God's promise and looked forward to their permanent home. His desire was for a homeland, a fatherland, a place where he belonged and where he and Sarah would be together again. Abraham longed to belong. And one day, he would.

There are many reasons for Abraham to call himself a stranger, but only one mattered: Abraham <u>knew</u> there was a better place for him. He realized he was a stranger.

Grasping Understanding

Abraham grasped what I was just beginning to understand after Mama's death: We don't belong here. This earth is not our home. We are strangers here, temporary residents, living in the in-between. What does that mean for us?

"Now those who say such things (that they are strangers and exiles) make it clear that they are seeking a homeland" (Hebrews 11:14 CSB).

First, we realize we are strangers here, destined for a better home. We're not meant for this world. God's promise for us is that we will have eternal life with Him and an eternal home.

Next, we must take action and seek this home. Seeking is a little different from what you might think. We all have those times when we diligently look for something. How many times have I lost my phone, only to discover it's right beside me (or even in my hand…)? And what about those pesky car keys that sneak out of my purse and end up in a spot they know they shouldn't be? We look and look and search and search until we find what we need.

But seeking? That is a strong desire for something. When you seek something, you yearn for it. It's a longing that needs to be filled. We seek the heart of our Savior, Jesus. We seek peace and contentment. We seek things that are highly valued but not easily obtained. We just can't grasp them. And yet, we keep on seeking. We don't give up.

Abraham was a hero of the faith who sought a homeland. He didn't just look for this homeland; he longed for it. We are the same.

Deep in our hearts, we know we don't belong. We want some-where that we fit in, a land and country to call our own. We yearn for a place to put down roots.

The writer of Hebrews tells us that Abraham "saw" the promises of God, and welcomed them from a distance (Hebrews 11:13). Imagine reaching out for a promise, and not quite being able to grab it. It's just out of reach. Abraham saw it and believed it, but he couldn't wrap his hands around it. Like a vapor.

But how did Abraham know about this future, better home-land? Jesus tells us that Abe "rejoiced to see My day, and he saw it and was glad" (John 8:56). Although Abraham didn't actually see the day of Christ, God must have told him something of its coming.

"Abraham by faith was granted a son Isaac, through whom the Seed (Christ) would come. How much of the messianic times God revealed to His friend Abraham is unknown. But it is clear that he knew of the coming salvation and he rejoiced in knowing about it and expecting it."[5]

Abraham lived with expectancy. He "saw" the day of Christ because he lived by faith. Even knowing that he didn't belong, Abraham continued to move forward, following God wherever He led. Abe didn't turn back, and he never settled.

> *Strangers and sojourners don't settle. They keep moving forward.*

Abe would not settle for what this world has to offer: riches and possessions (though he had these). Abraham would not even settle for death. He knew God offered more. Abe refused to be rooted in this world. He lived for the world to come. His true homeland. Strangers and sojourners don't settle. They keep moving forward.

We Are Sojourners

Like Abraham, we are sojourners here on earth, temporary residents. There is a deep longing in our hearts to belong somewhere, put down roots, and have a home. We want to find our place. But we don't belong here. We are strangers seeking a homeland.

When we realize we don't belong here, we understand we are on a journey to Heaven, our eternal home. This life and all the longings that come with it are part of our travels. They are stepping stones along the way.

With our hearts set on pilgrimage, our longings will lead us home.

> *Heaven is our true home and eternal homeland.*

Just as Abe meandered his way toward home, so too shall we. On our journey home, we will explore the longings of our hearts and how the hope of home can fill those longings. Despite our longing to belong, we realize that we don't. We will recognize Heaven is our true home and eternal homeland. We'll explore what it looks like to live as a stranger on this earth and rejoice in our identities as exiles. And we will learn to wait expectantly for our homeland to come.

At each stepping stone along our journey home, we will stop and reflect on where God is taking us. We'll pick up a small, smooth stone and slip it into our pockets, a reminder of God's promise of a better life to come.

• • • ● ● • ● ● • • •

Stepping Stone #1:

REALIZE:
We are strangers, longing for a better homeland.

REFLECT on God's Word:
Hebrews 11:8-10
Hebrews 11:16

RESPOND to the questions:

- How long have you walked with Jesus? Is your faith and obedience growing? Is it stagnant? What fears hold you back? Journal about your growth and your fears.

- When has your connection to Jesus caused you to feel like a stranger in our culture?

- Do you consider yourself a foreigner and a pilgrim on earth? How does this affect your priorities and actions?

Chapter 2

LONGING FOR IDENTITY

But in Heaven, every inch and ounce of who we are is perfected and totally filled.
 ~Mark Buchanan

In *How to Win Friends and Influence People*, Dale Carnegie said, "Names are the sweetest and most important sound in any language." Unless you hate your name.

For sixty years, I had avoided it like the plague. My dreaded first name. Because, unlike most people, my parents called us kids by our middle names. Crazy, right?

Sixty years. And then it came around and slapped me in the face. Sixty years I had been living by my middle name. Six decades I had been alive. Six decades called and known by the name of Ellen. And then, in an instant, my identity changed. Who or what did this? An evil person who knew I loathed my first name, so they plastered it all over social media? No. Nope. Not even close.

It was the Office of Motor Vehicles (OMV).

I can hear the skepticism in your voice: *Really, Ellen? How could they take your identity away?*

They can and they did. Because my driver's license expired. And no, they don't always send out reminders to renew your license. Silly, because the older I get, the more I FOR-get.

The office told me that since my license expired, I would need a bill or other document addressed to me, showing proof of residence. And, since the OMV links to the Social Security department, if the name on your Social Security card doesn't match the name on your license (mine doesn't, long story) you can't renew your license. Unbelievable.

Of course, I vented on Facebook, without ever mentioning the horrid first name. There was a lot of commiseration with all the bureaucracy. And then one small, itsy bitsy comment from my brother:

"Settle down Mildred!"

Well, the secret's out now!

Every document from that day forward had Mildred Chauvin on it. Insurance card, passport, you name it. Nothing like being in the doctor's waiting room, wondering when you'll be called to the back, only to realize they called you ten minutes ago. But you didn't answer because it was not the identity you've lived with for sixty years! Goodness! Who is this lady Mildred, and why do I have to be her? That's not who I am!

Funny as this story is, there was another, more emotional and heart-wrenching loss of identity. It began with a phone call early one morning.

Wake Up Call

The soft buzzing of the muted cell phone stirred me. Its persistence woke me from a deep sleep. I looked at the clock. Two a.m. My heart sank.

Mama! I grabbed my phone at lightning speed.

"Hello," I whispered, silently slipping out of bed, not wanting to disturb John unless it was necessary. And it may be. Two o'clock phone calls are usually an emergency.

"What's wrong?" I answered, seeing my brother's name on the ID.

"Are you awake?" he responded. Gulp. Yes, more awake now than ever.

"What happened?" I asked, my hand a death grip on the phone. *Please, Lord,* I prayed silently.

"Don't panic. Mama's okay now. But she coded a little while ago."

My brother Wayne's calm but urgent voice shook any remaining sleep out of my brain.

Coded. Coded!?

"What does that mean?" It seems I was the only one in my family who didn't get the "medical gene." I don't know a lot about medical terminology. The rest of them? They could be doctors. "Her blood pressure was sky high, and her oxygen went very low. The alarms woke Tammy (his wife), and she called the nurses' station. They stabilized Mama and will transfer her to the Cardiac Critical Care Unit."

It had been a hard couple of weeks. With my mom's stroke and extended stay in the hospital, I had been running back and forth: Louisiana to Mississippi and back home to Louisiana again. And again. Whatever it took. Finally, home for a break, and to catch up with life and work in Louisiana, I was tired. Worn down. And sleeping hard. Until the phone dragged me up to consciousness.

"Ok, I'll drive up first thing in the morning."

Arriving mid-morning, I found Mama's room through the maze of hospital corridors. Her appearance shocked me. Tubes and monitors covered her pale skin, a reminder of her frail state. The wires snaked around her, holding her prisoner. Just like the stroke was doing.

Soon, a cardiac doctor joined us to give an update on her condition. The white coat with a stethoscope draped around his neck screamed expertise and authority. I was wringing my hands, waiting to know his thoughts after seeing how fragile Mama appeared. I looked forward to hearing what he would say.

But not for long.

"Because of your mom's stroke and paralysis, she doesn't understand anything that is going on."

This fine doctor never spoke to Mama or looked her in the eye. He grabbed her face by the chin with one hand and roughly flopped it from side to side.

"See? She isn't responding. She has no control over her movements."

Ah, but this doctor was the one who didn't understand. I doubt he ever looked at her chart to see her name. He didn't know my mother. He probably erased her name from his charts!

Mama was awake, but not completely aware. However, I noticed something in her eyes. I knew her. And while she may not have understood the doctor's words, she knew he was not being respectful. She felt his ill-mannered attitude. And though Mama couldn't speak because of the stroke, the doctor did not get the last "word" with Miss Ann.

After he finished shoving her face around, my strong Mama gave that nasty doctor a "look," then turned her face and her back on him. She had no use for someone so rude. If the doctor had bothered to see my mom, if he had known her at all, he would have noticed the piercing look of disdain on her face. She snubbed him!

I turned and marched out. Tears threatened. Are they tears of heartbreak because of the doctor's treatment of my mom? Maybe they were hot, angry tears? Either way, I had to leave. Before a doctor lost his life.

That doctor erased and debased my mom.

Much like the Babylonians did to Daniel.

Daniel's Exile

We meet Daniel in the pages of scripture, in the book that bears his name. This book tells about the events of Daniel's life from about 605 BC when the deportation to Babylon began.

Nebuchadnezzar, king of Babylon, came to Jerusalem and besieged it. The city fell into the hands of her enemies, overtaken by the Babylonians.

After the fall of Jerusalem, the Babylonian army took the Jewish people captive. They deported the Jews, taking them into exile in Babylon. Daniel was one of these exiles. A teenager, Daniel was of royal lineage, intelligent and good-looking, without blemish. In other words, no physical defects. A perfect specimen, if you will.

Assimilation

The goal of the conquering Babylonians was to assimilate the Hebrew exiles into their culture. The Babylonian king wanted to absorb the Jewish people and make them a part of the Babylonian world. And why not? They would be great workers for the kingdom.

If the Jews assimilated properly, they would forget their homeland. They would eventually forget the ways of their God. They would lose their identities.

What means of assimilation did King Nebuchadnezzar use?

There were a variety of ways.

The king ordered his chief officials to teach the captives Chaldean (Babylonian) literature and language. This indoctrination included Daniel and his three buddies, Hananiah, Mishael, and Azariah. These young teens were supposed to forget their language and heritage and become an integral part of a foreign nation.

Nebuchadnezzar also gave them a daily ration of his choice, royal food. Hmmm. Royal food, fit for a king? Steak and lobster? And FREE? Well, except for the whole captive thing. Count me in!

However, Daniel resolved not to defile his body. He wouldn't eat the king's lavish foods.

"Mr. Overseer, please allow us to eat only the food that is healthier for us: vegetables and water. Test us for ten days and see if we don't look as good as, if not better, than those who are eating the king's rich foods." (Daniel 1:12-13, my paraphrase).

Daniel didn't want to contaminate his body and mind with impure food that didn't nourish. After ten days, if the king's officials couldn't see a difference, Daniel and his friends would be in big trouble.

Not to fear! Daniel knew what was good and healthy for his body. He, Hananiah, Mishael, and Azariah thrived with their healthier diet. After the allotted time, it was obvious they were more healthy than the other captives. They honored God by honoring their bodies. The king's rich food did not tempt them.

New Names, Same Identities

To further assimilate the Jewish exiles into Babylonian culture, they received new names. The Babylonians wanted to take away their identity. That was their goal: to strip the captives of their language, their culture, and their names. In Babylon, Daniel became known as Belteshazzar. I'm pretty sure that's the Babylonian version of Mildred.

In *The Daniel Prayer*, Anne Graham Lotz tells us about Daniel's new name. She says, "He was stripped of his identity and given a new name, Belteshazzar. The purpose of the new name, which was a tribute to a Babylonian god, would have been to destroy Daniel's loyalty and allegiance to his own God."[1]

As with the royal food, Daniel did not embrace his new identity. What an amazing young man he was. Daniel knew his Jewish roots, culture, and beliefs. He knew his God and did not give up his identity or his beliefs during the seventy years of exile. How?

Never forget Whose you are.

Daniel never forgot *Whose* he was. He belonged to the one true God. And it was to this God he prayed each day. Captivity didn't stop Daniel from his faithful life of prayer (Daniel 6:10-13). He longed for home each day of his life in exile. Every day, three times a day when he prayed, Daniel turned his face toward his beloved city, Jerusalem, where his people were from, those who knew his true name.

Standing Firm

Though he lost his given name, Daniel made a name for himself in captivity. Throughout his life in exile, he served under four kings. With God's help, he interpreted dreams for Nebuchadnezzar, which earned him a promotion. He explained the writing on the wall for Belshazzar. Finally, he stood up to King Darius' henchmen when they established a statute that said the people could pray only to Darius. Daniel did not obey this order, and the king's men threw him into the lion's den.

This distressed King Darius, who had taken a liking to Daniel. But Darius told Daniel, "Your God whom you constantly serve will Himself deliver you" (Daniel 6:16). Daniel left the lion's den with no scratches or injuries. God's angel closed the mouth of the lion. At this, Darius acknowledged Daniel's God, calling all the people to fear Him, the living God, who delivers and rescues in Heaven and on earth (Daniel 6:26-27).

But the most fascinating thing about Daniel is that no matter what new Babylonian name they gave him, people still called him by his God-given name of Daniel.

King Nebuchadnezzar called him Daniel. King Belshazzar knew him as Daniel. And King Darius, as well as his commissioners, knew him as Daniel and called him by that name.[2] They tried to give Daniel a new identity, but he was confident in who he was and Whose he was.

The book of Second Kings tells us more about the exiles initially deported to Babylon. They were captains, mighty men of valor, artisans, and Jerusalem's royalty and nobility (2 Kings 24:14-16).

The invading army left the poorest of the poor and took the best of the best. Daniel was one of these people.

He realized why he was an exile. He knew he was the best of the best. Not for his own gain, but for the glory of God. Daniel stood firm in his beliefs and his identity. He did not compromise. He would not assimilate into the pagan world where he lived. The Babylonians assumed he would capitulate. They didn't know Daniel. Rather than giving in, the opposite happened. Daniel took a stand and became a shining light for God. We can too, when we know our identity.

It's a struggle. There is a longing deep within each of us to belong to someone: a family, a people group, a spouse, or a community. We don't want to be the loner, the odd one out. We want to fit in and gain acceptance. We want to be known and liked. But, the world wants to assimilate us. They want us to become just like them. Never forget Whose you are. We don't get our identity from the world and its beliefs. As followers of Jesus, we find our identity in Him.

New Creation

"Therefore, if anyone is in Christ, he is a new creation; the old has passed away, and see, the new has come!" (2 Corinthians 5:17 CSB).

In addition to assimilation, the world will label us. The Babylonians considered Daniel and the other exiles "less than," nobodies, slaves. The world labels Christians in much the same way. They tell us we are unloving, narrow-minded, hypocritical, and not inclusive. However, when we are confident in Whose we are, we can be in the world without becoming a part of the world. We are brand new creatures in Christ, and we are who God says we are. Who is this "new" me?

Beloved. We are God's beloved[3] children. He dearly loves us. He adores and cherishes us. God esteems us. This means God thinks highly of us. And why not? He created us!

> *God thinks highly of us. How much more should*
> *we adore and worship Him?*

But think about it—If the Lord adores and admires us, how much more should we adore and worship Him? We are His beloved and adored simply because of who we are. We should praise Him because of who He is: Holy, worthy, all-sufficient. God should be our Beloved!

Chosen. Are you particular? I surely am! I'm particularly particular when I go grocery shopping. Apples can't have any bruises on them. I always check the expiration date on meats and canned goods. I am choosy. And so is God.

Before He created the world, God chose us (Ephesians 1:4). I love the way the New Living translation words it: "Even before He made the world, God loved us and chose us in Christ to be holy and without fault in his eyes." He loved us and chose us. We were more important to Him than creating the world. He picked us out from all others, for Himself, then made a place for us.

Known. Before God formed us in our mother's tummies, God knew us (Jeremiah 1:5). This is what God told the prophet Jeremiah. But I don't think it's a stretch to say that it applies to us as well. If God chose us before the foundation of the world, then He knew us before our conception. God intimately knows us, and He sets us apart for Himself.

He doesn't simply know us in the way we know our neighbors, giving them a wave as we pass them on the street. He knows us in all our private places, like someone who lives in our home with us. My husband can predict what my deepest thoughts are (most times!). That's how God knows us. He knows our every thought, word, and deed. Both the good and not-so-good! But even knowing all our thoughts doesn't change how He sees His children.

Righteous. No one is righteous (Romans 3:10). Why? Because righteousness is measuring up to God's standard, His excellence, and His holiness. And we always fall short.

It amazes me that, despite never attaining God's standard, I am declared righteous before Him. Me? In all my snarkiness? How can this be?

Because of Jesus. He exchanged His righteousness for our sins (2 Corinthians 5:21). Jesus was sinless. But at Calvary, He took on the sins of the world and gave His righteousness to those who trust Him for the forgiveness of their sins. Our righteousness comes through our faith in Jesus Christ.

Precious. Isaiah 43:4 tells us we are precious in God's eyes. He honors us and loves us. I am reminded of precious jewels: rubies, amethysts, emeralds. The owner would greatly treasure jewels like these. They are invaluable. That's what we are to God—precious jewels.

> ### *We are like precious jewels to God.*

Imagine God holding us in His great, powerful hands oh, so gently, so as not to hurt or wound us. Like holding a baby chick.

The most precious thing I've ever held was my grandson, who was born prematurely. In the NICU, I sat in a rocker and waited for him to be placed in my hands. He was so small! I was fearful of hurting that tiny little man. Gently, I traced his face with my fingertip, afraid that even this may scratch his translucent skin.

This must be how God holds us in His hands. Tenderly, because we are precious to Him.

Masterpiece. Ephesians 2:10 tells us we are God's workmanship, which denotes a work of art, or a masterpiece. The Greek word translated as "workmanship" is poiema. From this, we derive our word "poem." Imagine Shakespeare, Michelangelo, and other talented artists whose work transcends time. And us? We are God's masterpiece, a most beautiful poem. Our lives are a testimony to the greatest artist and creator of all time. Webster's dictionary calls a masterpiece "a supreme intellectual or artistic achievement."

This is who we are to God.

Forgiven. Past, present, and future. Those are all our sins that are forgiven. When Jesus died on the cross, our present sins (today's) were future. They had not happened—yet. But He died so that my today's sins are forgiven. "Neither the present nor the future. . . nor anything else in all creation, will be able to separate us from the love of God that is in Christ Jesus our Lord" (Romans 8:38–39 NIV). No matter how horribly we mess up, when we come to Him seeking forgiveness, He looks at us with love and says, "Go and sin no more. Your sins are forgiven."

These are just a few of my favorites. There is so much more to our identities in Christ Jesus. For example: His child, friend, free, equipped, saint, and forgiven. We are also heirs of God, recipients of a glorious "inheritance" (Ephesians 1:11.) As children of God, adopted by Him, we have a glorious bequest in Heaven. Eternal life with Jesus awaits us, along with a heavenly identity.

Better Identity

Wait. A heavenly identity? But I thought you said we'd have a new identity as soon as we made Christ Lord of our lives.

True. But we'll also have a new name when we get to Heaven. The book of Revelation tells us that Jesus will give three things to the believing saint who overcomes: manna, a white stone, and a new name (Revelation 2:17).

Just as God fed His people in the wilderness, Christ will supply hidden manna to those who endure persecution and stay pure from defilement. They are victorious because they don't assimilate into the culture and adopt worldly values. Sounds like Daniel, doesn't it?

The stone given to us is a stone or pebble, rather than a large boulder. In Biblical days, the stone was an admission ticket to an event or a ballot for a jury to cast a verdict. Black stones indicate guilt and white stones[4] acquit the innocent.

What a beautiful picture of what awaits us as overcomers and followers of Jesus Christ—an admission ticket to Heaven, and exoneration of the death penalty for our sins because of Jesus' blood.

But there is so much more. Along with our ticket, we'll have a new name written on our admission ticket. What does this mean? When we do a little digging, we find this verse in Isaiah 56:

"To them I will give in My house and within My walls a memorial, and a name better than that of sons and daughters; I will give them an everlasting name which will not be cut off" (Isaiah 56:5).

Our new name in heaven is everlasting.

A memorial with a name that will last forever. I'm reminded of a headstone on a grave. It marks our time here on earth—our birth date and the date we take our final breath. The white stone we are given preserves our names for eternity. As conquerors, Jesus gives us that name.

In Heaven, we will receive a white stone that will function as a memorial of sorts. Oh, what a memorial it will be! Inscribed with our new name, and the date "Forever", it will mark the beginning of the life we have been waiting for, ruling and reigning with Jesus. It's the start of the life we are meant to live, since the days of Adam and Eve in the Garden of Eden.

> *We are exiles longing for a better identity.*

What Jesus did for me after my mom's death, He will do for you, too. In my sorrow, Jesus embraced me and called me by name. He assured me I am known by Him, and that I will be fully known when I am finally home. We are exiles longing for a better identity.

Jesus knows us intimately. Realizing that our true identity comes from Him alone and we belong to Him, we can rest knowing that Jesus knows us completely. We can have confidence in who we are and Whose we are.

Daniel never returned to his beloved Jerusalem. He may have thought he would be more valuable in Babylon than in Jerusalem. Daniel lived out his life in a godless country and made a name for his God—the one true God who knows him by his eternal name.

Until we get our white stone with our new name, we are exiles with a better name awaiting us, and we live our lives for God's glory as we journey toward home. Like Daniel.

• • • ● • ● ● • •

Stepping Stone #2

REALIZE:
We are exiles longing for a better identity.

REFLECT on God's Word:
2 Corinthians 5:17
Revelation 2:17

RESPOND to the questions:

- Have you ever been called by the wrong name? How did it make you feel?

- God thinks highly of you. You are like a precious jewel to Him. What is your view of Him? How did you come to believe this about Him and know Him this way?

- How will you rejoice, knowing that Jesus has a special name just for you? That He knows you intimately?

Chapter 3

LONGING FOR WHAT WAS

If we want to prepare for our final destination, we should begin to worship God here on earth. Our arrival in Heaven will only be a continuation of what we have already begun. Praise is the language of heaven and the language of the faithful on earth.
~Erwin Lutzer

THE CALL CAME WHILE I was in the checkout line, unloading groceries. It had been four weeks since my Mama had her stroke.

"Ellen, it's Bebe. I just need to let you know that Mom is so tired, so very tired. I don't think you need to travel up here tonight, but she is just so very tired..."

Tears immediately flooded my eyes and began rolling down my cheeks. In the next few seconds, I was sobbing while trying to talk to my sister-in-law.

"Tell her..." I gasped, tears streaming.

"That..." Sobbing, gasping.

"I love her." Hysterical crying, gasping for air...

"Tell her...She's fought hard...That it's ok...I know she's tired."

The cashier overheard my side of the conversation and saw tears streaming down my face, snot dripping out of my nose, and drool trickling down the corner of my mouth. She pulled four or five paper towels from her roll and handed them to me.

I wiped away all the wetness (except for the tears that would not stop) and tried to pay for my groceries. My debit card didn't work. I was numb and stood there staring at the cashier. That sweet girl grabbed the card from my hand and swiped it as a credit card. She never said a word.

I thanked her with my eyes and rolled the grocery cart through the doors. The alarm sounded! Weeping, I looked back with a question on my tear-splotched face. She waved me through, never speaking. She just saw my heartache, my pain, and silently took care of me. That sweet clerk was the hands and feet of Jesus for me at that moment.

The next day, I called my brother to see how Mama was doing.

"Oh, she's doing better!"

But the sadness in his voice told a different story.

"The doctors say they've done all they can. You know she smoked all those years, and that damaged her lungs. They can't function properly because the stroke has weakened them. The doctors want to call in hospice. They say the best thing to do is make Mama as comfortable as possible."

Hospice. That's it, then. No more hope of recovery. How long did she have? How would we work this? Would she stay in the hospital until the end?

I packed my "go" bag and drove to Mississippi.

When I walked into her hospital room, Mama looked scared, tired, and drawn. She was subdued. Over the next several days, she slept a lot. When she was awake, she wanted to hold on to my hand—very unusual for my independent, strong mother. While I sat there holding her hand, I read scripture to her. The truth of God's Word comforted me as much as it calmed Mama.

Late one afternoon, I finally made the hard decision to return home. Leaning over Mama, I gave her a big hug and kiss, and told her I loved her. I turned, before she could see my tears, and practically ran down the hall.

Passing the nurses' station, I heard her. My Mama. Wailing "Bye, bye, byeeeeee."

I cried all the way to the car and down I-55. My imagination ran wild. Did she not want me to leave? Was she afraid she was dying? Was she scared? I didn't want Mama to be afraid. I didn't want her to be fearful. And I didn't want her hurting or suffering in any way. Her life had been hard early on. I didn't want her last days or weeks on earth to be hard, too.

I also berated myself. Why did I leave? Why didn't I go back? There was nothing so urgent at home that I couldn't stay another night or two. I was running away. I was the one who was afraid. Scared. Fearful. I was afraid Mama would die while I was with her, holding her hand. And I was afraid she would die when I wasn't with her. I was scared to stay and scared to go.

Four hours in the car, my face awash with tears, I wanted my Mama back. I wanted to go back to life before the stroke. Realizing I should have been there more, done more, what I wanted was a do-over. If I could turn the clock back, I would visit often, call frequently, and listen more. Mama and her wisdom will soon be gone, and I can never get back the time that I should have spent with her. I longed for what was and wanted a second chance. Grief, fear, and regret washed over me.

Did the exiles feel this way?

Returning Home

Seventy years! Finally free after seventy years! We haven't seen home, beautiful Jerusalem in seven decades. How much has changed? Will the city still be standing? And our homes? Will they still be there? What about the temple, where we met with God and saw His presence? What has happened to our glorious temple?

Hallelujah! We'll be home soon!

God promised His people, the Hebrew exiles, that they would return home after seventy years of Babylonian captivity (Jeremiah 29:10). But only a remnant returned to Jerusalem. Many Jews had become comfortable in their captivity and were reluctant to leave. The country of their captors was now their home. The Babylonians had allowed them to establish businesses and build houses (Jeremiah 29:5-7). Others, however, returned home, not knowing what to expect.

After the Persian king Cyrus defeated Babylon, the Lord moved Cyrus' heart to allow the Jewish captives to return to their homeland. Off they went, on pilgrimage, heading home. With joy and anticipation, they set out. They couldn't wait to see their homes and their city.

But what they found was desolation. The conquerors demolished the city wall. Only a pile of stones remained. The enemy's invading army burned the ornate palaces and destroyed anything of value. Ash heaps, that's what the exiles saw. And the temple? Their most holy place of worship? Torn down, flattened, nothing but rubble (2 Chronicles 36:19, 2 Kings 25:9)

Where do you start? How do you begin rebuilding?

With the pile of rubble and stones. One stone at a time.

Rebuilding the Temple

Their top priority was to rebuild the temple and re-establish worship of the one true God. After much hard, grueling work, they built the foundation of the altar. The people, led by the priests, reintroduced sacrifices (according to the law). They celebrated the Festival of Tabernacles. What joy and excitement filled their hearts. What a celebration it must have been! Singing songs of praise and worship, raising hands in thanksgiving! Joy-filled laughter spilled from their mouths as they cheered the completion of the altar. The people were delighted, thankful, and hopeful! But not everyone.

Many of the older men who had seen the original temple in all its glory wept loudly (Ezra 3:12-13). Worship and wailing co-mingled. My heart grieves with these old gentlemen, knowing the pain. Nothing is as it used to be. You can't go home again.

These sweet older gentlemen didn't just cry, they moaned and groaned in sorrow. Their hearts shattered into a million pieces. Like me, I imagine they had tears streaming with snot and drool dripping. They lamented the former temple.

"We have caused all this! The magnificent temple is gone, nothing but ruins. All because we abandoned our God..."

The men remembered what used to be—the splendor, beauty, and size of the temple that Solomon built. Their hearts shattered over "what was." This new temple would not match the glory of the destroyed temple. Joy and sorrow collided, leaving them feeling a bit of nostalgia.

It was there in the twinge in their guts, the tightness in their chests. A dull ache that couldn't be soothed, a deep sadness was present in their hearts during this most joyful time. It's a sense of longing whose source is hard to identify. A yearning deep within for…what? There's an empty hole within them, seeking to be filled.

This hole in their souls, the deep soul-wrenching pain, is it for the worship traditions long forgotten? Or for the precious memories of the glorious temple? Nostalgia always brings an ache. And rightly so. The word is from the Greek "nostos" or homecoming, and "algos" or pain. We've all experienced it occasionally. The pain of homecoming.

Only to find the house vacant. Life changes. Divorce leaves holes, death leaves empty spaces at the dinner table. Life's circumstances leave ragged edges like wrapping paper torn and tossed aside. The past is gone and uncertainty lies ahead.

They felt disheartened, dismayed, and discouraged. And I imagine they felt more than a little regret. You see, it was their unbelief and disobedience that sent them into exile (Ezra 5:12). God had used the Babylonians as agents of judgment against His people.

"Why didn't we listen? Why didn't we trust Yahweh more? We didn't obey and follow Him. Why?"

They were heartbroken over the chaos they caused. Longing for the former days in the grand temple, they ached for a second chance to be the people God intended them to be. They feared what the future would bring.

Consequences of Longing for What Was

What happens when you long for what was?

The door to opposition opens. Satan knows when we are at our weakest. That's when he throws fiery darts of chaos into our lives.

The returning exiles ran headfirst into resistance from the Samaritans, who had been living in Jerusalem for the last seventy years.

It was now their home. The returning Hebrews were nothing but foreigners to them. Pilgrims passing through. The Samaritans hindered the rebuilding efforts of God's people. In addition, there was a new governor in the region who refused to approve the construction of the temple (Ezra 4:17-21). Every chance they got, the opposition stalled the work of rebuilding.

The Samaritan's intimidation tactics put fear into the hearts of the Hebrews (See Ezra 4). Who knew what consequences they would face if they disobeyed the governor? The resistance they faced threw them into confusion.

Fearful, and discouraged by the conflict, overwhelmed at all that needed to be done, they stopped work on the temple. But they did begin restoring their own homes. Their lives, destroyed by the exile, needed to be rebuilt. Meanwhile, the abandoned temple lay in ruins. For about sixteen years, it stood unfinished and ignored.

Rather than a joyous homecoming with a new temple to restore their worship practices, they became paralyzed. As far as the temple was concerned, they froze and became immobile.

Gazing at Doodlebugs

When negativity of this magnitude falls on me, I keep my head down and focus on what is immediately in front of me, remembering with fondness all the better times. I don't look up at all the work to be done. I only work on something I can finish. Small projects. Little things that don't matter. Max Lucado calls this looking at doodlebugs.

In his book, *God's Story, Your Story*, Max recounts the time he took his grandchildren to the zoo. He wanted to surprise them with the magnificence of the jungle section, so he told them to keep their eyes down. And that's when it happened—they spotted a tiny doodlebug.

Oh, he tried to get them to look up and see all the wild animals, but:

"No, they focused on the bug. There we stood, elephants to our left, lions to our right, only a stone's throw from hippos and leopards, and what were they doing? Playing with a doodlebug."[1]

The returning exiles were looking at the doodlebugs of their circumstances, rather than appreciating their freedom and homecoming. They took their eyes off the prize of a new temple, a place of worship, and a place where God's presence would dwell.

> *Longing for "what was" enslaves us.*

Looking back with regret, they didn't do what needed to be done. Looking ahead with fear, they only worked on their homes and not the Lord's house. They focused on what was in front of them, working on a smaller project they could complete.

Longing for "what was" enslaved them and prevented God's people from moving forward and finishing His temple.

All progress stopped. They were stuck. They needed help.

That's when the prophet Haggai arrives, giving them a hefty dose of truth and reality.

Time to Rebuild

"Then the word of the LORD came by Haggai the prophet, saying, 'Is it time for you yourselves to dwell in your paneled houses while this house lies desolate?'" (Haggai 1:3-4).

The Lord, via Haggai, lobbed a truth bomb at the returning exiles.

You rebuild your own houses, but neglect Mine? What is most urgent?

God was reminding them of how important His home—the temple—is. It symbolizes His presence with the people. As the temple goes, so go the people. If the temple lies in ruins, decaying, so will the people's relationship with Him. It was imperative to rebuild the temple. The people had been away for seventy years. Many became assimilated into the Babylonian culture. Many had forgotten or didn't know their God. Their hearts needed to be reunited with the Lord, worshiping Him.

God stirred the spirits of the returning remnant. After laying untouched for so many years, they began rebuilding His house. But with one major difference: they were not alone. God was with them and understood how they felt.

"Who is left among you who saw this house in its former glory? How do you see it now? Is it not as nothing in your eyes?" (Haggai 2:3 ESV).

> *God sees our tears and knows our hearts.*

God saw the opposition and discouragement. He saw their tears and knew their heart. And through Haggai the prophet, He encouraged them.

I like to paraphrase God's encouragement in Haggai 2:4-5 like this: *Take courage and work. I'm with you! My Spirit remains among you. Don't be afraid!*

Though He had exiled the Jewish people, God brought them home again. Even though it seemed God had deserted them, He was ever in their presence. Though it seemed He didn't care about them, He was faithful to encourage them to move forward. It's never too late to begin again. With God.

Future Glory

This was His reassuring promise to them: One day, the glory you will see in this temple will be so much more than the glory in the previous temple (Haggai 2:9).

More splendid than the temple Solomon built? How is that possible? The people saw the small, plain altar and wondered how it could be more majestic. After all, Solomon imported cedars from Lebanon to construct the temple. And he overlaid the cedar with gold (1 Kings 6). Solomon built a beautiful temple. What could be more glorious?

Ah, it's here we get a glimpse of the new covenant. The flesh and blood Messiah will be in the new temple. He will adorn the temple built in Herodian times (Matthew 12:6).[2] Jesus, the Word of God made flesh, will be in this temple. He will walk, talk, and teach here. Jesus will proclaim liberty to the captives (Luke 4:18, Isaiah 61:1) in this rebuilt temple.

Haggai wasn't just speaking about the physical temple in Jerusalem. His reference to a more glorious temple speaks to the Holy Spirit of Jesus. Believers receive His Spirit the moment we place our faith and trust in Him. The very second we make Jesus our Lord and Savior, God sends the Spirit of His Son to live in us. The apostle Paul tells us *we* are temples of God, and that the Spirit of God dwells in us (1 Corinthians 3:16, 6:19). Our bodies are a temple of the Holy Spirit who is in us.

This future glory is also a reference to the Church.[3] Jesus' people united in Him, our cornerstone. Isn't that glorious?

Ultimately, Haggai is speaking about the millennial temple. At that time, "the Lord God the Almighty and the Lamb are its temple" (Revelation 21:22). God and Jesus will be the temple. There won't be any need for the sun, because Jesus is the Light. When that day comes, we will be with Him forever, worshiping Him. Now that's something to look forward to!

Glorious!

Press On

From time to time, we all long for life before the struggle. Before the death, before the divorce, job loss, or any number of devastating circumstances, we want to go back to our old normal. Regretting that we didn't make the most of what was, we want things back the way they were. We don't belong in this new normal, but we also don't belong in the "what was."

We can fondly remember the way things were, marking and memorializing it. But we can't stay stuck in the past or camp in our grief. To grow, we must move forward in faith. Don't covet the past. Look ahead. Cultivate an attitude of expectancy at what God will do. Live with hope.

Focusing with regret on what was and fearing what lies ahead keeps us from envisioning and longing for the future God has for us. God told the exiles, "'For I know the plans that I have for you,' declares the LORD, 'plans for welfare and not for calamity to give you a future and a hope'" (Jeremiah 29:11). The Lord promised this even before they went into captivity.

Grief and suffering, hardships and heartbreaks, will grow us if we allow it. So often we resist the pain. We mourn for the past, not leaning into the pain or the lesson. We become the walking wounded.

Poor pitiful me.

We want a grand temple instead of humble new beginnings. We want what we had, instead of looking ahead to all Jesus has for us.

Paul gives excellent advice in Philippians. He tells us to press on! Forget what is behind you. Reach forward to what is ahead of you (Philippians 3:11-14).

Remember our buddy Abraham? He kept looking ahead to a better country. Abraham didn't settle.

And Daniel. He kept his eyes on the Lord. He stood firm, knowing there was a better identity ahead of him.

And our ragtag group of returning exiles? Eventually, they looked forward. They rebuilt the temple with God's help. It took a while, and it was hard work, but they did it!

Let's not wallow in our grief. That's where I was when Jesus interrupted my misery and regret. He reminded me that there is no condemnation for those of us who are in Christ. Jesus assured me that my Mama loved me then and still loves me. She's saving a place for me.

God has plans for you. Strangers, pilgrims, and exiles don't give up or turn back. They know there is a better future ahead (John 3:16, Psalm 16:11, 17:15). Allow yourself to dream again (Psalm 126:1). Keep moving forward.

· · · ● · ● ● · · ·

Stepping Stone #3

REALIZE:
We are pilgrims longing for a better future.

REFLECT on God's Word:
Ecclesiastes 7:10
Psalm 16:6

RESPOND to the questions:

- What kinds of emotions do you imagine the returning exiles experienced as they made their way back to the land God had promised?

- Are you pressing on, or camping out in your grief or suffering? How can you move forward with an attitude of expectancy at what God will do?

- Are you enslaved by the past, longing for what was? What steps can you take to begin again?

Chapter 4

LONGING FOR HOME

*Home isn't a place I pursue or a destination I achieve. Home is
Jesus. And resting in who He is, right here.*
  ~Michele Cushatt

P RAYER JOURNAL ENTRY:
    *Thursday 7/28/11 Going to Braxton today to see Mama. Very
tired and weepy.*

I pulled into Mama's driveway, hearing the crunch of gravel under
my tires. Then I saw it—my brother Wayne's car. I didn't realize he
would be here this early. He met me outside wearing a grim look on
his face.

These words greeted me: "It's not good." My stomach knotted.
My oldest brother Steve had called Wayne home sooner since he lived
closer. Why? Why didn't Steve tell me it was so bad? I would have
been more prepared.

Then I understood: Steve wasn't prepared, either. Grief also overwhelmed him. Steve is a big, burley guy, kinda gruff looking. Meeting him in a dark alley would leave you frightened out of your wits.
But deep down inside, he's a big ole teddy bear with a big ole heart.
Seeing his Mama lying paralyzed on her hospice bed was more than

his big heart could handle. Steve didn't want to tell me any bad news over the phone. He needed me and our brother Wayne there with him. We needed each other.

Once inside, Steve explained a little more to us.

"She was having trouble this morning. Bebe and the hospice nurse determined it was time for a very small dose of morphine to ease her breathing. And to help with her panic. We know her time is getting close because her body is shutting down."

It was only a matter of time. The knot in my stomach tightened.

I sat next to her bed, studying her small, wrinkled hands. Their roughness testified to the fact that these eighty-five-year-old hands had worked hard through the years. As a young child, she had picked cotton in the fields with her sharecropper father. She always told us picking cotton was the hardest work she'd ever had to do. But her daddy rewarded her with praise.

"You're the best cotton pickin' cotton picker I've ever seen!"

I rubbed her hands gently, hoping she could feel the love flowing from my hands to hers. Glancing out the sliding glass doors, I watched the geese swimming in the small pond. The reflection of the trees on the water was fading with the sun. My brothers and sister-in-law were hovering quietly, waiting. Soon it would be time for me to move and let Wayne say his goodbyes.

My heart was breaking. I had so much to say, so much I wanted to tell her. But the lump in my throat blocked all the words. Even if I could squeeze them out, would she hear me? Her first dose of morphine had left her unconscious, each breath labored.

Did we make the right decision? To bring her home with hospice care and stop medical treatment? Deep down inside I know we did, but oh Lord, how I'm struggling with it now.

Her hospital bed stood in place of the long wooden dining table. She would have wanted it that way. Her special spot was at the table, watching the hummingbirds feed and the antics of the squirrels. We shared so many meals there. Memories are in every stain and scratch of the light oak. But no more. Silently I waited, while the oxygen machine screamed disapproval at me.

Click, hisssss. "You sssshould have been here more."

Click, hisssss. "You sssshould have come home more often."

How many times had Mama waited for me to come home? Now, filled with regret, I silently waited for her...to go home.

I walked a few feet into the kitchen area to warm our supper. It may be a long night. We would need to eat. Bebe and Wayne were bedside, talking softly.

"Look, she's smiling!" Bebe said. My brother Steve's wife, Bebe, who is a nurse, had been keeping a close eye on Mama. A few seconds later she added, "That's just reflex."

Wayne called me over. Hurrying, I wanted to see the smile on Mama's face before it was gone. Instead, this.

"She's gone."

"But...how do you know?"

"Because, baby, she stopped breathing..."

And just like that, the waiting was over.

Mama was home.

Overwhelmed by Grief

In the weeks that followed, I struggled. Grief overwhelmed me. I could not believe my mom was gone. It didn't seem right. Each time reality hit, it felt like someone sucker-punched me in the stomach. *How long will it hurt, Lord?*

"My soul weeps because of grief; strengthen me according to Your word" (Psalm 119:28).

That's me. My soul is weeping with grief. *Strengthen me, Lord!*

Driving along in heavy traffic, I would look into the cars next to me. All these people are going about their lives and doing normal things. Work continues without a blip. Don't they know? Can't they see? My life has changed drastically! How can people keep going along, living life, just as if everything is the same? Grief engulfed me.

Of course, I Googled "grief" to see what I could find out about my state of mind. Depending on what I read, there are five to seven stages. The reality phase says, "This pain is unbelievable; the purest pain you have ever known." Yes, I agree. I'm pretty sure I am experiencing all the stages at once. That is the storm of grief.

Soon, I found a website with devotions for Christian grievers. That was me! It asked something I'd never thought about. We celebrate when someone graduates from high school or college. Why don't we celebrate when a loved one "graduates" to Heaven? Oh, we have "celebrations of life" but usually they are more somber. Why couldn't I rejoice that Mama was in Heaven, healed and whole?

One thing I know; God will see me through this. He will strengthen me through His Word. And yet I struggled to get up in the mornings for my quiet time, reading scripture, and praying.

Season of Loss

To add to the angst, John and I were in a season of loss. Two weeks after Mama passed away, my ninety-seven-year-old father-in-law died. He lived a good long life, but it was still a heartbreaking time. And that was just the beginning.

After Pop, we had another death and then another. Four funerals in four months. At that point, we had a reprieve of six months. And then it began again. Three more funerals!

A well-meaning friend told me, "Ellen, this is just for a season. Hang on!"

It was a looooong season. Within a year, we attended seven funerals, many at the same funeral home.

Can you imagine?

I could just picture the funeral director's face when we walked through the door yet again.

You're back? Come on in, make yourself at home. You know where everything is, don't you? That's your people we have here today? They're in Parlor B, the one dedicated to your family.

Nothing says "Welcome Home" like a funeral director who knows your name.

Like a hard driving rain, grief and sorrow pelted us. Or so it seemed at the moment. Would it never end?

It's during seasons like this when we realize there is more to God's kingdom than just our little world. I was grieving, yes. But I was also wallowing in my own little pity party.

How does one recover from so great a loss?

Like Abraham, by continuing to move forward.

Like Daniel, standing firm in faith.

Like the remnant of exiles, by re-establishing worship with God by their side.

I began with gratitude. That's what I needed in my life. Slowly, I started thanking God for all His blessings during Mama's passing.

Thank You, Lord, that:

-I arrived at Mama's at 5 p.m., she passed at 7:30 p.m. I'm so thankful I got to hold her hand and talk to her before she passed from this earth.

-My brothers and I were facing a hard decision. Should we turn off her oxygen? It was keeping her alive, but by somewhat "artificial" means, something Mama didn't want. Thank You, Lord, You took away this decision.

-I had brought food, and we needed every single bit. Thank You, Lord, for Your provision!

Gratitude showed me all the ways God had been with me. Even when I didn't see Him or feel His presence.

Gratitude brought me back to prayer. Slowly, my prayer life shaped up. Remembering others who are going through a season like mine, I lifted them to our God of all comfort. I poured my heart out to God, telling Him how much I missed my Mama. Through my grief, I prayed and screamed and praised Him.

Prayer brought me back to His Word. I began immersing myself in the scriptures. My focus returned (thank You, Lord!), enabling me to read and grasp many things. But one stood out to me like a glaring neon sign.

Light and Momentary Afflictions

I wasn't the only one who had struggled these past few months. My mom also struggled. Her stroke took away her ability to talk. And oh, how she loved to talk! Every Saturday morning, she would make phone calls to all the kids.

"Hey darlin', hope I'm not calling too early."

"No ma'am, I just finished coffee and I'm about to go dig in my flower beds. I'm planting petunias. Will they come back next year?"

"Well, darlin', they may. Are you planting or setting out?"

"Um, I don't know. What's the difference?"

Turns out, planting is starting a plant from seed. Setting out is planting a seedling or young plant. Oh, and did you know that hot water sets the stain? And if you gargle with warm salt water, your sore throat goes away. And Vicks Vapor Rub is the go-to home remedy for a chest cold.

Yes, the stroke brought many trials to my sweet Mama. She could not move the way she wanted or talk to any of us. Mama tried to say words, but they came out garbled. She wanted to communicate, but only a few words came out of her mouth, frustrating her: "Yeah, yeah, yeah. Right. Riiiiight!"

The Apostle Peter tells us we will suffer, but only for a little while (1 Peter 1:6, 5:10). And Paul says our troubles are light and momentary (2 Corinthians 4:17-18). James tells us that testing produces patience and we should consider it all joy when we have trials (James 1:2-3).

Do you see it? The way they describe our troubles?

> *Our troubles are temporary. There is a beginning to the suffering, but there is also an end.*

We will suffer only for a short time. Our troubles are temporary. There is a beginning to the suffering, but there is also an end.

Our troubles are light. This means they are insignificant, not heavy. They are easy to bear. Oh goodness, how? Because we have Jesus walking with us. Our friends are praying for us. And we remember our trials don't last forever.

Momentary. Fleeting. Only lasting for a brief period.

But what do these troubles produce for us? Patience. An eternal weight of glory. This glory is what we will have when we are face-to-face with Jesus. And it's how we should see our trials and troubles here on earth: temporary. We can see suffering as temporary when we focus on Jesus and being together with Him forever in Heaven.

My mom's troubles were temporary. They ended the moment she breathed her last breath on earth, and Jesus welcomed her home. Now, she could rest in His presence.

Better to Depart

If I could ask her, I would say "Mama, how do you see all this? What's your point of view now?" I'm pretty sure she would feel the same way Paul did:

"But I am hard-pressed from both directions, having the desire to depart and be with Christ, for that is very much better; yet to remain on in the flesh is more necessary for your sake" (Philippians 1:23-24).

Like Paul, I'm sure Mama would like to stay with all her kids. But considering the stroke and her faith in Christ, she desired to depart and be with Him.

The Greek word for "depart" is analúsō, meaning "to loose."[1] The ancient Greeks used the word to indicate loosening an anchor, so the ship could set sail. Many commentators suggest another definition. It is taking up, or loosening, your tent stakes to move on. Remember Abraham? He was constantly loosening the stakes of his tent to move around.

Paul compared our earthly bodies to "tents" (2 Corinthians 5:1). By trade, Paul was a tentmaker, so he understood their short-lived nature. Ancient Israelites primarily used tents as their home. The fabric was cloth woven from goat hair. Strong for a time, but the weather and constant moving eventually degraded even the sturdiest fabric. Tents are temporary and wear out.

Our bodies are the same. Since the curse of sin entered the world, our physical bodies won't last forever. They are temporary. We are sojourners wandering through this temporary, earthly life desiring permanence. That's what my Mama would tell me.

"Well, darlin', this ole body of mine just cain't go anymore. I'm tired and worn out. I need rest. It's better for me to leave."

Better to depart.

Paul Knew Heaven

How can I know it's better? How did Paul know?

Because he was there. Paul saw Heaven.

Jesus brought Paul up to Heaven to give him divine revelation. He was "caught up into paradise" (2 Corinthians 12:1-4). It was in the highest heavens where Paul heard things so astounding he could not tell them here on earth. In Heaven, Jesus was sharing His knowledge with Paul. He was teaching Paul great things,[2] not so that Paul could boast. The things Paul learned helped him spread the good news of Jesus. We can trust Paul's teachings because The Greatest Teacher taught him!

One thing Paul saw with his own eyes was that Heaven is better.

If I had my "druthers" (as in 'I'd rather...'), my preference would be to have my Mama with me. A girl needs her mommy.

Mama would tell me it's better to take down her worn tent because now she is in her permanent home with Jesus. Paul tells us the same thing. He flat out says that his preference (his druther!) is to be out of his body (his earthly tent) and be at home with the Lord (2

Corinthians 5:8). Paul is longing to reach his destination—home in Heaven with Jesus.

Not only would Paul rather be at home with Jesus, but he says it would be better by far than remaining here. He had a good old-fashioned dilemma. It would be better to leave and be with Jesus, but remaining was necessary for the benefit of the believers in Philippi. They needed spiritual growth and knowledge, and Paul could help them. Even so, Paul knows that our ambition "whether at home or absent, (is) to be pleasing to Him" (2 Corinthians 5:9). There was no choice. By staying and ministering, Paul was pleasing the Lord. By remaining, he was being obedient.

Paul saw Heaven as his true home. Yet he came back to earth and lived as an exile, stranger, and teacher extraordinaire. Because of Paul's teachings, I know Mama is finally home.

It's better for her than anything we could offer here on earth. All the hugs and love we can give are nothing compared to being home with Jesus. Yes, the stroke caused great suffering for my sweet Mama. But when she walked through the gates of Heaven into the arms of her Savior, I have no doubt she said, "It was worth it!"

I was homesick, just thinking about her there. I ache to be with her one day. But my tent still has a lot of life left in it, God willing.

Only God can determine when it is time for us to depart this earth. He's given us purpose and work to do here. We remain, even when every longing in our hearts is to be in our better home with Christ. Until then, we move on and finish the race (Philippians 3:14, 2 Timothy 4:7).

Grief is a Slow Process

Mama, I miss you! My heart cried out. Then, I imagined her fussing at me:

"Honey, you just need to straighten up, wash your face, and follow the Lord."

Time to put on my big girl panties and mind my Mama.

Follow the Lord. But where was He leading? All I could feel was my grief. My mother's death threw me into a pit so deep I didn't think I could ever crawl out. I wasn't sure I could claw my way to the surface and see the light of day again. Only my sweet husband realized the depths of my sorrow. He asked if I needed to talk to someone—a pastor or a counselor. And tell them what, exactly? That my heart is ripped out of my body? That my grief is a literal heartache?

As I prayed and followed the Lord, I realized some things. When we are in the depths of grief, we can't see past our pain. We need to allow ourselves time to grieve.

> *Grief is a long, winding road with many twists and turns, hills and valleys.*

Oh, I know, I know. Life goes on, the world keeps turning, and you only get three days of funeral leave. But don't tamp down those feelings you have. Don't push them aside. Give yourself time and space to grieve. Visit with your family. Talk about your loved one. Those memories you made together? Remember them! Look through pictures and share your stories. It's okay to grieve.

Know that grief is a long, winding road with many twists and turns, hills and valleys. Many days you won't be able to see the forest for the trees.

Grief is a slow process. The deeper the love, the deeper the pain. The more you feel at home with someone here on earth, the more you will long for them when they've gone on to their eternal home.

Grief will blindside you when you least expect it. You may be in the grocery store looking at bunches of bananas and suddenly burst into tears. Shoppers around you will give you strange looks, wondering if they should call the EMTs. But the thing is, those bananas reminded you of homemade banana pudding. It tasted just okay, but that banana pudding had cups full of love as the key ingredient.

Grief rears its ugly head at the most inopportune times. Know this will happen. Know this is normal. And don't worry about what the people in the produce section think about your flood of tears.

In your grief, cling to Jesus. Reach out, grab the hem of His cloak, and hang on for dear life! Hold on to Jesus with all you've got! Grief narrows our focus. Make sure you expand your focus wide enough to include Christ. Read His Word, even though it may not soak into your soul. Read devotions written specifically for those who are grieving. Pray, even if you have no words. Groan if you must (Romans 8:26). Grab Jesus and don't let go! His grace is sufficient. It is a supernatural, enabling grace that will carry you (or drag you) through the darkest days of your life. It is amazing grace.

Finally, follow the Lord. He loved you into this sorrow and He will love you through it. Ask Jesus to take you by the hand and walk with you, leading you toward home. That's a prayer I'm sure He would be happy to answer!

Randy Alcorn[3] says it best:

> "Home for me was always wherever Nanci (*his wife*) was. That means my house is now less my home and Heaven is more. As much as I miss her, it's a good trade off, because I now feel like Nanci did in her final months on earth—ready to meet Jesus. If death comes today or next month or in a year or a few decades from now, I'm ready too. 'For we know that when this tent we live in—our body here on earth—is torn down, God will have a house in Heaven for us to live in, a home he himself has made, which will last forever' (2 Corinthians 5:1 GNT)."

> *Grief is a longing for home.*

As my heart began healing, this is what I realized: Grief is a longing for home. All our longings lead us home. Our troubles here on earth are temporary. Our pains and struggles are nothing compared to being in the presence of Jesus.

Jesus taught me, like He did Paul and like He will teach you, that Heaven is a better home. And He is there to welcome us home.

· · ● ● · ● ● · ● ·

Stepping Stone #4

REALIZE:
We are sojourners longing for our better home.

REFLECT on God's Word:
Philippians 1:23
2 Corinthians 5:8

RESPOND to the questions:
- Have you walked through grief or suffering so deep you were floundering? How did Jesus bring you through it? Journal about that time and your feelings.

- Do you realize your suffering is temporary? How can you begin to think about the end of your pain or trial? What will that look like?

- Do you long to be at home with Jesus? What does this reveal about the loyalties of your heart?

Part 2

● ● ● ● ● ● **●** ● ● ● ● ●

On Our Journey Home

We

Recognize Heaven is Home

Chapter 5

WHY LEARN ABOUT HEAVEN?

God limits the happiness and pleasure we have now precisely so we might not become attached to this world or dependent upon it or fearful of leaving it (dying), as well as to stir in our hearts a longing and yearning and holy anticipation for what is yet to come.

~Sam Storms

T HE DEVOTION PUZZLED ME. I purchased it at a women's conference to supplement my morning Bible reading. Fighting against throngs of women swarming the book tables, I saw the perfect devotional book. It was all about hope!

Hope was exactly what I was looking for at the beginning of the new year. I had waited months to begin the book I purchased in October. After all, it was a 365-day devotion that started on January 1st. My friends laughed at me when I told them I would wait to read it.

"Why wait? It looks like a great devotional!"

"I know, but that's just how my brain is wired. I may peek at the pages and see the devotion for my birthday, but I'll hold off reading it until the first of January."

Orderly and process-driven is what I am. It's the way God made me. I wanted a fresh start in my quiet time in January, so the book remained closed until then.

But when I finally opened it on New Year's Day? It surprised me. It was not at all what I expected.

Each day in January, the reading was about rejoicing when a loved one, who knew Jesus, passes away. I couldn't understand how a person would or could celebrate the death of a spouse, parent, child, or friend. They were gone, leaving you with a broken heart. Rejoicing over the death of someone I loved was not normal for me.

The funerals I had been to did not have that type of rejoicing. I vividly remember learning funerals were sad occasions as my seven-year-old self watched my daddy.

Walking past a long box, I saw the man lying in it. Why wasn't he moving? Why was everybody looking at him? Couldn't he wake up?

We found a seat and waited for the church service to begin. It was odd. All the pastor did was talk about the man in the box. We didn't sing hymns or open our Bibles or do anything like regular church.

Head down, hair shielding my face, I snuck a peek at Daddy. He was crying! Hard, choking sobs. I figured out the man in the box had died. He would never wake up. It made my daddy very sad.

Death and funerals equaled sadness and tears for me. For the next couple of decades, I avoided them.

"Honey, Aunt Ramona died last night."

"Aww Mama, I'm sorry. Give everyone a hug from me. Tell them I'm sorry I can't come home for the funeral." No way was I going to travel and sit through something so sad.

The devotion I purchased at the women's conference boggled my mind and made me rethink all I thought I knew. Each day, I read a scripture that explained more about the passing of those who are in Christ Jesus. These passages told me the death of one of God's saints (believers) is precious in His eyes (Psalm 116:15). John 17:24 told me that Jesus wants us to be where He is, and He is waiting for us. The apostle Paul, in his letter to the Philippian church, said that to live is Christ and to die is gain (Philippians 1:21). The most touching verse for me was Revelation 21:4 which reads "and He will wipe away every tear from their eyes; and there will no longer be any death."

In Heaven, God is going to wipe away all tears and destroy death forever. What's not to celebrate?

The more I read, the more I realized the ladies who wrote these devotions knew and believed in their hearts that Heaven is real. For them, it was normal to rejoice when a loved one who is a believer dies. Why? Because when a believer dies, they are going to an actual place. It's called Heaven.

By the end of January, reading all the devotions that celebrated the death of Christians, I embraced this message and recognized we can and should rejoice for those who have gone there before us.

Six days later, my daddy died.

> **Heaven is real and we need to learn about it.**

God, in His infinite wisdom, had prepared me for Daddy's death. He knew I was a person who liked to know things. God knew I wouldn't open that devotional book and begin reading until January. The devotions about rejoicing and celebrating our loved one's death prepared me. Yes, I was sad. However, after reading that devotional when I did, I understood one fact that changed the course of my life. Heaven is real, and I needed to learn about it.

God had prepared me by teaching me about Heaven. This stirred a passion in me to learn as much as possible about the truth of our home there.

Growing up in the church, I believed God's Word. But I had received little teaching about Heaven. Oh, we rejoiced at John 3:16 and eternal life and how to get to Heaven, but teachings on the what and where of our eternal home were few. There was a gap between my head knowledge and my heart knowledge. But what a difference knowing and learning can make!

Our Hearts Can't Love What Our Minds Don't Know

"The heart cannot love what the mind does not know."[1]

What an important truth! Therefore, if our minds don't know about Heaven, our hearts can't start loving it.

When John and I first started dating, I didn't know too much about him. He was nice. He was cute. He was polite.

"Hold on, I'll get the door for you."

"Oh! Thank you!"

The more I got to know him, the more I liked him. Especially when he exceeded my expectations.

"Hey Ellen, just calling to see how you're doing. How about we go out to a movie tomorrow night?"

"Nooo, can't. Sorry. I have some sort of stomach virus. Food is coming up, and uh, you know, going out the other way, too."

"Oh," I could hear the *Uh Oh* in his voice, "Uh, can I do anything to help?" *Please let her say "No", please let her say "No."*

"I hate to ask, but would you get some anti-nausea stuff and bring it to me? You don't have to, but..."

Gulp. "Oh, sure. Be there in a few minutes!"

Yep, the more I learned about him, the more love took hold. My heart followed my mind. I knew he was a good man. God loving. Very respectful. Polite, polite, polite! He always opened the door for me! What a gentleman! My heart said, "He will be a wonderful husband."

Maybe it was love at first sight for you? One of those soul-mate relationships? You knew immediately this was the person for you. Still, the deeper the knowledge you have about them, the deeper the love.

Similarly, it is imperative to learn about Heaven so that we can love it with all our hearts and look forward to it. That sounds strange, doesn't it? Because to look forward to it, we must die. And no one wants to die, myself included.

Dying to Get to Heaven

There are no two ways about it. Death stinks. As I sit here writing this, we've just come from my neighbor's funeral. He was only 70 years old. His wife looked forward to a long retirement with the love of her life. My neighbor's children expected him to see their children grown and married. His untimely death cut short all their dreams.

In her eulogy, his daughter brought tears to our eyes when she said, "Isn't it something that the hardest day for us here on earth is the most glorious day for my daddy? Because he is finally able to go home."

Death hurts so much because we love so deeply. The greater the love, the greater the loss.

But we can't speak about Heaven without first addressing death and dying. And for Christians, the possibility of death is a win-win situation. Think about a hard diagnosis, such as cancer. Our chances are slim. But if the Lord heals us on earth, we have more time with our loved ones! WIN! If He heals us by bringing us home to live with Him forever, also a WIN! Our death is hard for our loved ones left behind. There's a hole in their hearts the size of Texas. However, our Creator designed us to live forever with Him. Win-win.

> *For Christians, the possibility of death is a win-win situation.*

There is also a fear of death. As Christians, it may not be so much the fear of death, as fearing the manner of our death. What's your preference—a fiery car crash or peacefully dying in your sleep at the ripe old age of eighty-five or so? I know what I would choose! Fear is another reason we should learn what happens when we die. Knowledge conquers fear! Now, let's learn.

Simply put, when believers die, they go immediately into the presence of Jesus (Philippians 1:22-23, 2 Corinthians 5:6-8). Rather, our souls go to be with Jesus. Our bodies stay behind. Temporarily. A Christian's death isn't permanent, their life is. Scripture depicts death as a type of sleep until our reunion with Jesus.

*The tombs were opened, and many bodies of the saints who had **fallen asleep** were raised.* Matthew 27:52

*This He said, and after that He said to them, "Our friend Lazarus has **fallen asleep**; but I go, so that I may awaken him out of sleep."* John 11:11

*But we do not want you to be uninformed, brethren, about those who are **asleep**, so that you will not grieve as do the rest who have no hope.* 1 Thessalonians 4:13

*Then David **slept** with his fathers and was buried in the city of David.* 1 Kings 2:10

It's a beautiful thought, isn't it? The second our hearts cease to pump life-giving blood here on earth, we are in Jesus' presence. The second we pass away from this life, we are more alive than we've ever been. We are absent from the body, but present with Jesus. He welcomes us home with open arms.

Our souls go to be with Jesus, while our bodies remain here, "sleeping." I think of it kind of like a big ol' bear hibernating for the winter. Our bodies are waiting for the season of "spring" when they will be together with our souls.

We are all going to die. For those of us who love Jesus, we will look forward to being with Him and to our eventual resurrection. In simple terms, this is when our body and soul are together again.

Learning about Heaven in order to long for it and to love it, is to know our physical bodies will die, to accept this fact, and to wait for that day with anticipation. Not anticipation that ties your stomach in knots, because of the anxiety of a painful death. But the great anticipation of seeing Jesus face to face.

Oh, happy day!

With All Your Heart, Soul, Mind and Strength

Scripture tells us to love the Lord our God with all our heart, soul, mind, and strength (Mark 12:30). We use our minds to teach us the things of Heaven. We study Heaven with all our strength. Then, the funny thing is, our hearts will follow our minds. The reality of Heaven will seep into our souls. We will believe in it and know with the certainty of faith that it is real.

The apostle Paul explained to the Corinthian church that we become what we behold (2 Corinthians 3:18). This means that if we continually look upon Jesus and learn about Him, we will become progressively more like Him each day. And one thing Jesus knew: Heaven is real, and it is His home. He stepped down to earth to fulfill His Godly purpose of dying, to save the world from sin and death. But He knew that each day on earth, He was on a journey back home to His Father. So as we behold Jesus and become more like Him each day, we recognize Heaven is our home.

At the ripe young age of sixty, I met my half-sister, Honey. She was my dad's third child. Although I had known of her, I had no recollection of ever seeing her face to face. Immediately after we found each other I learned three things about Honey: She loves Jesus, has never learned to swim, and when she dies and enters Heaven, she is going to run and jump into the River of Life!

Just over a year later, she passed away. My heart was broken for my loss. But when I thought about Honey swimming in the River of Life, I rejoiced! She was doing something she had always wanted to do.

> *Knowing and loving Heaven causes us to focus on the eternal.*

When we know Heaven, we can look forward to being there. We can rejoice when our loved ones in Christ die. Knowing and loving Heaven causes us to focus on the eternal more than things of this world.

In the words of this beautiful old hymn:

Turn your eyes upon Jesus,

Look full in His wonderful face,

And the things of earth will grow strangely dim,

In the light of His glory and grace.[2]

Earth is temporary, Heaven is eternal. When we learn about and love eternity and Heaven, our focus won't be on the material things of this world. Even our grief and trying circumstances will fade when compared to the eternal life we long for.

What Heaven Isn't

When you think about Heaven, what comes to your mind?

Often our views of Heaven come from some not-so-biblical places. You've probably seen movies that portray God as a cigar-chomping, amiable, old man out to save the human race. Maybe your view of Heaven's angels comes from the irreverent portrayal of the Archangel Michael. He is a cigarette-smoking, sugar-loving, angel on earth. The tagline? *He's an angel, not a saint.*

Books and movies often portray Heaven as a place where people who have died turn into angels, sit on clouds, and strum their harps all day. This couldn't be further from the truth. When Christians die, they don't become angels.

Angels are not resurrected or reincarnated people. They are NOT humans. Angels are ministering spirits to God's people (Hebrews 1:14). They cared for Jesus when Satan tempted Him (Matthew 4:11).

God created angels (Colossians 1:15-17), and they are God's special messengers to carry out His plan. They brought messages to Daniel (Daniel 9:20-23) and Mary (Luke 1:26-38). They also serve God by encouraging His people, as they did for Paul (Acts 27:23-24).

Angels are agents in administering the affairs of the world, and they care for the needs of the followers of Christ (Hebrews 1:13-14, Matthew 1:20; 18:10, Acts 7:30). Angels are not members of God's family, as believers are. They are finite, unlike Jesus, who is infinite (Hebrews 1:1-14).

Some people consider Heaven will be boring. In Mark Twain's **The Adventures of Huckleberry Finn**, Huck says "She [teacher Miss Watson] went on and told me all about the good place. She said all a body would have to do there was go around all day long with a harp and sing, forever and ever. So I didn't think much of it."[3]

Why won't Heaven bore us? In Heaven, everything is fresh, and all things become new! Heaven is where everything is as it should be, and we are finally and fully home. It is where we find (as Mark Buchanan says) "that mysterious something we never found down here. All that has held us back here on earth—the weariness, the fear, the dullness, the brevity, the poverty—vanishes."[4]

Work in Heaven won't be the tiresome drudgery we are accustomed to here on earth. It will stretch us in good ways, and be fulfilling like we've never known it to be here. As Randy Alcorn suggests:

"The Bible's picture of resurrected people at work in a vibrant society on a resurrected earth couldn't be more compelling: We're going to help God run the universe (Luke 19:11-27). Work in Heaven won't be frustrating or fruitless; instead, it will involve lasting accomplishment, unhindered by decay and fatigue, enhanced by unlimited resources. We'll approach our work with the enthusiasm we bring to our favorite sport or hobby."[5]

No, Heaven isn't boring. And neither is God. He is the One who created humor and laughter. He is the one with a great sense of adventure. God promises that we'll laugh and "experience endless pleasures in Heaven."[6]

Imagine being reunited with friends and loved ones who have passed away. Do you see the smiles on their faces? Is your face creased with a grin that stretches from here to eternity? That's Heaven.

Imagine meeting the saints of old and asking them questions. I'm sure I will have a list for Abraham, Daniel, Peter, and Paul! Purpose will fill us and we will sit at the feet of Jesus, basking in His glory and love. Oh, the joy and wonder it will bring to our souls! Forever!

What is Heaven?

First, let's settle this. It's a fact. Heaven is real. Why? Because the Bible says so. In the first verse of the first book of Scripture, we are told that in the beginning, God created the heavens and the earth (Genesis 1:1). If we believe the earth is real because God created it (and we live here), we must believe Heaven is real because God created it. We believe (by faith) that we will live there.

Heaven is also God's dwelling place. Solomon identifies it as such in 1 Kings 8:30. It is where God's throne stands:

The LORD is in His holy temple; the LORD'S throne is in heaven. Psalm 11:4

The LORD has established His throne in the heavens. Psalm 103:19

Thus says the LORD, "Heaven is My throne and the earth is My footstool. Isaiah 66:1

Heaven is God's home, His throne room, and it is from there that He operates:

The LORD looks from heaven; He sees all the sons of men; From His dwelling place He looks out on all the inhabitants of the earth." Psalm 33:13-14

Although we know Heaven as God's home and His dwelling place, we need to remember that God is spirit (John 4:24), and He is omnipresent. This means that He is everywhere, at all times. Neither time nor space can contain Him. Though Heaven is God's dwelling place, He is always with us!

Heaven is also called paradise, a blissful place with unending delights for us. Jesus told the thief on the cross, "Today you shall be with Me in Paradise" (Luke 23:43). Paul also calls Paradise the Third Heaven (2 Corinthians 12:2-4). The original Greek is **parádeisos,**[7] meaning garden or park. I can't imagine a lovelier place to spend eternity, can you?

Where is This Place?

Heaven is where Jesus sits at the right hand of His Father.

It is also where those who have placed their faith and trust in Jesus go when they die.

This is where things get a little complicated. There is a "Now" and "Later" aspect of Heaven.

Now, Heaven's location is in the "heavenlies." Where that is exactly, I can't say. But this "intermediate state" is the transition period after life on earth and before our resurrected bodies. When Christians pass away, they are immediately in Jesus' presence, with intermediate bodies. They are in the present Heaven, in the heavenlies.

Randy Alcorn discusses the common misunderstanding that when we die, we'll go to "the Heaven where we'll live forever. Instead, we'll go to an intermediate Heaven. In that Heaven—where those who died covered by Christ's blood are now—we'll await the time of Christ's return to the earth, our bodily resurrection, the final judgment, and the creation of the new heavens and new earth." [8]

This is the "now" aspect of Heaven.

Later, when Heaven opens up and the New Jerusalem comes down, there will be a new Heaven and a new earth (Revelation 21:1-2). At this "later" aspect, we will have our glorified, resurrected bodies. There will be more on this in Chapter Eight.

With both the intermediate state, or present Heaven, as well as the new Heaven and new earth, we will be in the presence of Jesus. This is what we long for and look forward to now—being with our Savior!

In chapters five through eight, when I speak of longing for Heaven and loving Heaven, I am talking about the later aspect—the new Heaven and earth.

Why Must We Learn This?

One huge reason Christians should learn about Heaven is that Satan doesn't want us to know! Satan wants us to believe the lies that Heaven is boring, with nothing to do but strum harps and sit on clouds. Why does Satan want us to think like this? So we won't anticipate it with joy. Satan doesn't want us to "long for the resurrection and the endless beauty God has in store for us."[9]

That old devilish fiend doesn't want us to know the truth about Heaven. He doesn't want our hearts to love what our minds have learned. Satan knows we will share this truth with others. If there is only one thing this book accomplishes, I pray it's that you, dear reader, will come to know and love Heaven.

Satan wants us to cling to all our earthly possessions with clenched fists. He wants our hearts tied to the temporary, not dwelling on glorious eternity. He would rather us longing to remain here on earth than longing to belong in Heaven.

We learn about Heaven so we will look forward to it with hope. The Bible tells us we are not to grieve as others who have no hope (1 Thessalonians 4:13). Paul tells us in Thessalonians not to be uninformed about those who have died, so we won't grieve as those who don't believe in the eternal life offered by Jesus. The hope we have is in Jesus and a life spent with Him. This is our hope: Eternal life, with Jesus, in our new home.

If we don't know the things of Heaven—where it is, what it is, and how the Bible describes it—we won't learn to love it. We won't embrace it as our Christian destination.

Our hope tells us we have an eternal home. Our hope tells us we will be reunited with our loved ones—those who have placed their faith in Jesus to take them home to Heaven when they die. Oh, what a glorious day that reunion will be! But without knowing all we can of our eternal home, we won't look forward to that day with great expectancy.

> *We learn about Heaven because we long to belong, and Heaven is where true believers belong.*

We learn about Heaven so we understand it is real and recognize that it is our true home.

We learn about Heaven because we have a longing in our hearts to belong. Heaven is where true believers belong. We learn about our home so we will long for it.

My desperate prayer when my mom had her stroke was: "Lord, prepare me! Prepare me like You did when Daddy died!"

I wasn't ready for Mama's death. Letting go and losing my Mama would break my heart.

But God didn't prepare me. I had to walk through the hard and heavy grief of losing my mom. You know what? My God of all comfort was right there beside me. Jesus walked with me, and carried me, especially when I stumbled. He strengthened me.

And after she died? He taught me more and more about my better home which prepared me for the next time grief strikes. Now, I can love Heaven and look forward to it.

Don't wait until you suffer a significant loss to learn about Heaven. Don't wait until you are in the middle of grief. Prepare now by learning to love Heaven.

• • • ● ● • ● • • •

Stepping Stone #5

RECOGNIZE:

Heaven is real and we should learn all we can about it.

REFLECT on God's Word:
2 Corinthians 3:18
Luke 23:43

RESPOND to the questions:

• What things are you beholding (gazing upon)? Are they temporary or eternal?

• What are your perceptions of Heaven? Do you think of it as an actual place? Do you believe it's boring? Why?

• What do you most look forward to about Heaven?

Chapter 6

WHY LONG FOR HEAVEN? I LIKE IT HERE!

My hope is that this life is not all there is. This life is like preparation for what is coming next, and what is coming next is something so glorious that the Bible says minds can't conceive it, eye has never seen, your imagination could never enter into all that God is preparing for those who love Him.
~Anne Graham Lotz

P UDGY LITTLE HANDS SLOWLY chose a colorful piece of cardboard.

"No, not that one. Not yet. We're looking for all the pieces that are straight on one side."

Teaching my grandchildren the art of putting together a jigsaw puzzle (even a fifteen-piece one) was fun!

"Granny, how long will this take?"

"Granny, this will never look pretty like the puppies on the box!"

They couldn't wait to see the finished picture. They couldn't imagine the end product would look as beautiful as the picture on the puzzle box. Only, it didn't.

"Granny, what happened? There's a hole in the middle."

Right in the center of the puzzle, there was a void, a great empty space. We were missing one piece. One last piece that would complete the puzzle.

There was a gaping hole in our whole.

That's how my heart had been feeling these past several months since Mama's death. Filled with grief, I found it difficult to imagine the other side of the pain. There was a hole in my heart. I miss my mom, aching to see her again and longing to hear her voice. Homesickness overwhelms me, knowing I'll never go back to Mama's house again.

Yes, I'm sure that's what the ache and void in my heart is—missing Mama. Such an earth-shattering loss in my life. But that doesn't explain the other times I've felt it. The ache, the emptiness, the sense of lack. There have been many occasions when I've felt an unexplained hollowness in the depths of my being.

Sehnsucht Longing

This emptiness is more than grief. It's the feeling that washes over me every so often. It's usually when there is a crispness in the air, with crimson and amber leaves floating to the ground. Farmers are burning the sugarcane fields, taking me back to my childhood. We raked leaves into huge piles. Walking a few feet back, we would run as hard as we could, arms pumping, and jump right in the center of the leaves. They scattered, only to be raked up again. Eventually, my daddy would light a match, burning the pile of leaves.

This ache, this yearning, is so acute it brings tears to my eyes. It's a joyful sorrow that takes my breath away. Similar to the time we saw Old Faithful bursting forth in all her steam and water-filled beauty. The hot springs geyser shot water straight up for hundreds of feet, looking like a cloud. Rainbows formed in the steamy water. It was breathtaking. It left me wanting. Like there is so much more, something better out there, just beyond my reach. It's a yearning for...something.

I discovered this bittersweet ache has the name. *Sehnsucht.*

Sehnsucht is a German noun that means "longing." It is the inconsolable longing in the human heart for a far, familiar, non-earthly land one can identify as one's home.

This hole in my heart is an aching for my Heavenly home. Far away, but familiar. Not earthly, but will one day be the new Heavens and earth.

> ### *God created us to long for Him and Heaven.*

We can't help longing for our true home. God created us to long for Him and Heaven. Christians know this deep desire. It is eternity, and God placed it in our hearts.

Eternity in Our Hearts

> "He has made everything beautiful in its time. He also has planted eternity in men's hearts and minds [a divinely implanted sense of a purpose working through the ages which nothing under the sun but God alone can satisfy], yet so that men cannot find out what God has done from the beginning to the end" (Ecclesiastes 3:11 AMP).

The writer of Ecclesiastes puts a name to this emptiness. He identifies this void as a hole that can't be filled here on earth. It is eternity. He tells us that God has set eternity in our hearts. God planted it there, and every day it grows deep roots within us. It's an ache for eternity in our hearts that causes our longings. But let's face it, it's a difficult thing to understand eternity and Heaven. My brain can't grasp the truth of eternal life while my heart grieves here on earth.

Like my grandchildren trying to envision the beauty of a finished puzzle without the benefit of the box, I struggle to imagine Heaven and life forever. There are gaping holes where beautiful family pictures should be. Those we've loved are no longer here. They have left us behind. After a long journey, they are home, safe and sound. They can exhale and rest in eternal peace; all of us here on earth are still traveling. They are worshiping at the feet of Jesus; we are merely playing worship music. We're not jealous of them. Not exactly. We're just longing to be home with them.

What would that be like?

Imagining Heaven

Just because it's hard doesn't mean we shouldn't try to visualize Heaven. Randy Alcorn suggests it is a good practice to imagine Heaven. He said we cannot anticipate or desire what we cannot imagine:

"That's why, I believe, God has given us glimpses of Heaven in the Bible—to fire up our imagination and kindle a desire for Heaven in our hearts. If God didn't want us to imagine what Heaven would be like, He wouldn't have told us as much about it as He has. I believe we should fuel our imagination with Scripture, allowing it to step through the doors that Scripture opens."[1]

When circumstances and grief overwhelm us, it's time to look at cold, hard facts: the truth of God's Word. So, let's begin with scripture to spark our imagination about what eternity is like, and why we should long for it.

God gave us our imagination—let's use it to envision Heaven.

Heaven Our Inheritance

Can you envision a life-changing inheritance being left to you?

Well, you have one. It is Heaven.

We are "adopted" into God's family. As His children, we are His heirs and co-heirs with Christ (Romans 8:17). We receive the promise of our inheritance by hearing the truth of scripture and believing in Christ (Ephesians 1:13).

Many passages in the Bible mention the bequest to us. In Ephesians 1:11, Paul tells us we received this inheritance from God because He chose us. God gives us the Holy Spirit as a down payment for our inheritance. What a wonderful, loving Father!

In Colossians 3:24, we are told to work in our daily jobs and lives as if we are working for the Lord. Our reward will come from Him. What is that reward? Our inheritance!

But what is the inheritance?

Heaven is our Promised Land.

For the Old Testament saints, it was the Promised Land of Canaan. For all of us New Testament saints, it is Heaven and everything God has promised us in salvation. Heaven is the land we will inherit, living there forever (Psalm 37:29). Heaven is our Promised Land!

Peter gives us more facts about our inheritance (1 Peter 1:4). First, he tells us it is imperishable, which means it is not subject to breaking down. It is beyond the reach of change and decay. Therefore, it lasts forever. Spiros Zodhiates says it isn't like our bodies that will die, but "something that the believer receives in this life and will continue to have after this life is over."[2]

Our inheritance is also undefiled, or pure. It is free from stains or blemishes. Think about things we may receive as an inheritance here on earth: Great-grandma's china, the beautiful crystal bowl your mom always used to serve Christmas dinner side dishes, the silver plated flatware used for special occasions. All lovely items. But cracks, chips, or tarnish have affected many pieces. Blemishes mar their purity. But, our heavenly inheritance is pure and holy. No stains! Lovely!

Do you like fresh flowers? I do! I love them so much I try to grow a few varieties each year. Zinnias are my favorite since they tolerate heat and drought. They are also great cut flowers, lasting days in a vase of fresh water. But eventually, they fade and die.

Our inheritance is much better than zinnias. Peter tells us it will not fade away. There is an interesting word usage here. The original Greek for "fade away" is *amárantos,* which is a word similar to the lovely flower Amaranth. Hmmm, I wonder if the Amaranth is a long-lasting cut flower?

Finally, Peter tells us that our inheritance awaits us in Heaven. Our inheritance is Heaven, and it is the eternal life we will receive in Heaven. We have a better life that is forever, as well as eternal salvation in Jesus.

Paul tells us that the Holy Spirit is the down payment of our inheritance.[3] The Holy Spirit is a pledge or guarantee of more to come.

When Jesus was comforting His disciples in John chapter 14, before He was about to ascend to Heaven, He told them He would ask God to send a Helper. In the original Greek, the word for Helper is "parakletos."[4] Our Helper (or paraclete in English) is someone who comforts and encourages us. He walks with us throughout this life. The Holy Spirit is with us during our suffering to strengthen us. He is our Counselor and He will be with us forever (John 14:16). That's good news!

Our Helper aids us in discerning truth from error. He is the Spirit of Truth (John 15:26). He also will teach us all things. Imagine, you only need two things to study and understand God's Word: The Holy Spirit and a Bible!

The Holy Spirit brings to mind things we've learned from Him. Are you one that says, "I just can't memorize scripture"? Yes, you can! You have a Helper! Even when you don't realize you have memorized verses, your Helper will remind you.

Driving home from work one day, I was having a debate with the Lord. My church asked me to serve as chairperson of a committee. I didn't want to, nor did I feel qualified. So I told God every single reason I couldn't say yes. You know what He did? He answered me with scripture (that I didn't know I knew). He countered every "no" with a passage from His Word that told me He has equipped me! I lost that debate, needless to say.

The Holy Spirit provides all this for us. He supernaturally enables and empowers us. The Holy Spirit gives us "divine strength needed...to undergo trials and persecutions on behalf of the divine kingdom."[5]

With Him, we can withstand suffering and trials. With the Holy Spirit's leading, we can and will do God's work. The Holy Spirit transforms us. He is the guarantee of God's promise that God will finish His work in us and bring us home to Him.

Imagine this: If the Holy Spirit is just a down payment, how much more abundant will life be together with Christ in Heaven? It will be more than we could ask or imagine.

The pledge of the Holy Spirit also brings us hope for Heaven.

The Hope of No More

Specifically, the hope of *No More*. We find this hope in the book of Revelation:

"and He will wipe away every tear from their eyes, and there will no longer be any death; there will no longer be any mourning, or crying, or pain; the first things have passed away" (Revelation 21:4).

In Heaven, there is no more crying. No more tears dripping out of our eyes, slipping slowly down our cheeks because of sorrow. But what about happy tears? Hmmm, that's a good question. I think if we cry happy tears in Heaven, they will flow all the time!

What causes our crying here on earth? Mourning, grief, and sorrow. We mourn over those we love who have died and left us here on earth. But it is more than the sorrow of death. Many times we mourn the loss of our dreams or opportunities that have passed us by. Broken relationships make us sad and we grieve the loss. We mourn the loss of our abilities—either as we age or because of illness. But one day, that sorrow and grief will all be gone. In Heaven, there is no more death or dying. And no more funerals! None! And those countless tears will be wiped away by God Himself.

We grieve and are sorrowful over all the sins we see in this world. Every day we read horrendous headlines about drugs, murders, break-ins, theft, kidnappings, child pornography, and trafficking. We worry about someone breaking into our home at night and harming or killing us. In Heaven, we'll no longer need to worry about these things. Why? Because there will be no more sin or evil in this world (Revelation 22:3). None. Nada. *No more.*

Hard to imagine, isn't it? This world is full of evil because Satan is in it. But when Jesus returns to conquer sin and death, He also overcomes evil. Satan's eternal destination will be hell, the lake of fire and brimstone, where he will be cast away forever (Revelation 20:10). Satan's eternal banishment means there is nothing unclean in Heaven (Revelation 21:27), and nothing unclean will enter Heaven. Glorious!

There is no more pain in Heaven. The empty ache that shows up from time to time will never pierce my heart again. Any physical afflictions will be gone. No more sickness, dying, or death. Oh, think of it! No more cancer. No more diabetes. No more disease. No taking cholesterol medicine, because there is no more high cholesterol! And simply the best for some of us (of a certain age) is this: no more colonoscopies!

In Heaven, we will have no more fear. No more phobias. Our stomachs won't flip-flop when we are in the highest altitudes, flying, or any kind of travel. Anxiety won't cause us sleepless nights, because nothing will induce the heart-stopping, sweaty palms of anxiety in us! We will be alive forevermore, so there will be no more fear of death because there is no more death (Revelation 20:14)! My goodness, I may even go spelunking in the darkest cave because I won't fear dying in the depths of the earth surrounded by bats.

And here's a beautiful picture—no more darkness. No night and no need for lamps. Why? Because the Lord God will be our light. Jesus will be our lamp. He will shine on us and be our light forever (Revelation 21:23, 22:5).

Several times I said there will be no more death. Yes, I repeated myself. No, it isn't age related. It's just something that bears repeating! Jesus conquered death!

Imagine, a world with no more!

Our Hope

And when grief grips our hearts here on earth? Remember this. We do not grieve as those with no hope (1 Thessalonians 4:13). Those who do not believe in Jesus and don't place their faith and trust in Him are hopeless. The saddest funerals in the world are those without the hope of Jesus. But not for us who know Him! This is the expectation and assurance we have:

Hope of salvation (1 Thessalonians 5:8). This is not merely wishful thinking, hoping to be saved. It is the hope that salvation gives us. It is a past, present, and future hope: (1) Past—we have been saved from the guilt and punishment of our sin; (2) present—we are being saved from the power of sin, and (3) future—we will be saved from the very presence of sin when we are home with Jesus.

Hope of righteousness (Galatians 5:5). We know we can't make ourselves righteous (or holy). No one is righteous, not one (Romans 3:10)! Our hope is in God, who will complete His work in us. And thank goodness He will complete what He started! If I had to finish all the work needed to complete myself, I would become weary.

"Working for my righteousness is hard. I can't do it anymore!" This would be my mindset. And it's true. We cannot maintain our holiness or righteousness on our own. We can't produce perfect righteousness in our lives. We need help. And God has provided us with help by the Holy Spirit. Through the Spirit and by our faith in Jesus, we wait and have confident hope that God will complete our righteousness in due time.

Hope of eternal life (John 3:16). God loves us so much that He sent His Son to pay for the crime of our sins. Whoever believes in Jesus will live forever with Him! Growing up, I heard this preached. But I did not internalize what it meant until I matured, both as a woman and as a Christian. We will live forever with Jesus, no matter what may come our way here on earth. This is our confident hope!

Hope of my eternal home Jesus prepares (John 14:3). Jesus has our rooms ready! He has prepared our eternal home and is waiting for us.

Hope of glory (Colossians 1:27). Glory? What is this hope of glory that we will have? Oh, it won't be a glory like God has, that's for sure!

God's glory is what He is, and we can boil that down to being holy and perfect. The glory of humans is "what they are meant by God to be, though not yet perfectly attained."[6] We have not yet reached our completion in God. And we won't until we are home with Him. Our hope of glory is the hope of "blissful perfection"[7] which is the destiny of all of us who will live with God in Heaven.

Now that is something we can hold on to—the hope of glory. What God means for us to be. Blissful perfection. Do you know what bliss means? It is complete happiness, paradise, or Heaven. Complete happiness, because Jesus completes us. And it is our inheritance in Heaven. This is the missing piece of the puzzle. That one piece, when snapped into place, completes the whole, wiping away any empty spaces, longings, and the angst of not being complete. Jesus holds this piece of the puzzle. He will finish us in due time. He will complete what He started (Philippians 1:6). Blissful perfection is our inheritance because we live with God in Heaven.

> *One day the messiness of this earthly life will be completely and perfectly redeemed.*

There is hope that one day the messiness of this earthly life—the sorrow, the tears, and the pain—will be completely and perfectly redeemed. Not only will there be no more tears and crying, but the constant longing in our souls will be filled. We will know with complete clarity His purposes for us.

God is our God of hope. He will fill us with joy and peace, as we believe. And His Holy Spirit? By His power, we will overflow with hope (Romans 15:13)!

Christ in us is our hope of glory. There is no hope but in Jesus (1 Timothy 1:1). He fills all the empty places. Some of that glory, that completeness, that hope, will be filled here on earth and will spill out from our lives into the lives of others. And the rest? We will see the fullness of Jesus' filling in Heaven. That's something to look forward to, amen?

Our Grief in the Here and Now

What does this mean for us in the here and now?

It's kind of like waiting for retirement. On our worst days, can we hang on? Can we endure? Yes, because we know retirement will be here soon. And it will be outstanding!

This is the hope we can cling to now—that one day we will be complete and mature, lacking nothing, all our longings filled...with Jesus!

> *God gave us this ache for Jesus, for eternity, for home.*

We grieve for our loved ones who have gone before us, but we know in our hearts they are more alive than they've ever been. They are sitting in the Son light, next to Jesus. We miss them. Our hearts ache with the longing to be with them. More than that, we long for the day when we can sit with Jesus and talk to Him face to face. God gave us this ache for Jesus, for eternity, for home.

Until then, we have hope and a confident assurance that one day the hole in our hearts will be filled. We are certain of the inheritance waiting for us, and we can't wait! With help from the Holy Spirit, we envision Heaven, because as good as things are here on earth, it is nothing compared to what is to come!

Knowing the reality of Heaven, we look forward to it and long for it. Because it's paradise (Luke 23:43). And it's home.

Imagine that!

· · · ● ●· ● ● · ·

Stepping Stone #6

RECOGNIZE:
Heaven is better than we could ask or imagine.

REFLECT on God's Word:
Ecclesiastes 3:11
1 Thessalonians 4:13

RESPOND to the questions:
- Have you ever felt a bittersweet ache in your heart? When and where? What do you believe caused the ache? Do you think it was God?

- What do you imagine Heaven may be like? How can you begin using your imagination and God's Word to paint a picture of Heaven in your heart?

- Which of the "hopes" listed (salvation, righteousness, eternal life, eternal home, glory) do you look forward to most? Why?

Chapter 7

WHY IS HEAVEN HOME AND WHOSE HOME IS IT?

We live here as strangers and aliens. Our roots, our citizenship, and our hopes are anchored in the soil of the city of God.
~Nancy Guthrie

LATE AGAIN!

Wednesday night Bible studies are a challenge. I work thirty miles away and am usually rushed to get to class on time. I hate to miss even a small part of the current study, ***Heaven*** by Randy Alcorn. Barreling into my house, I gobbled my dinner, grabbed my Bible, and ran out the door again.

Screeching into the parking lot on two wheels, I hopped out of my car and sprinted to the Fellowship Hall. I slid around the corner on the freshly waxed floors, hoping to slip into the classroom before the lesson started.

I almost ran headfirst into the closed door. Oh no! I needed to be extra quiet now, so I wouldn't disturb anyone.

Slowly, I turned the knob and pushed. It wouldn't budge! Someone had locked the door!

I was locked out of Heaven!

Many people will have this same problem. They believe they are going to Heaven by being a good person, working hard, giving money to their church, and even going to church regularly. But it isn't about what you do. It's about Who you know (Jesus) and the gift He has given (salvation).

Sadly, not everyone will accept this gift of eternal life. Jesus gives us this gift, but we must take it and unwrap it! Those who don't won't spend eternity in Heaven with Jesus.

Make sure you and those you love won't be locked out of Heaven. Make sure that you choose Heaven as your home.

Whose Home Is It?

Billy Graham once said, "We're probably going to be surprised at some people who will be in Heaven. But we also may be surprised when we get to Heaven to discover who isn't there!" Yes, some people will be locked out of Heaven!

Currently, there is a pervasive belief in our world that everyone ultimately goes to Heaven, that Heaven is the default. This is called Universalism. It is a doctrine that teaches all people will be saved. Universalists believe everyone will go to Heaven, regardless of what they believe or how they've lived their lives.

At funerals, we often hear the officiating person say, "We know they are in a better place now." Sure, it may just be politeness, rather than saying "Pretty sure he's rotting in hell now!" But most people believe when someone dies, they are in a better place.

This is a hard truth to face: Not everyone will end up in Heaven. The Bible tells us that the gate to life and Heaven is narrow, and few people find it (Matthew 7:13-14). Jesus even tells us that not everyone will enter the kingdom of Heaven (Matthew 7:21-23).

The major argument for Universalism is that a good and loving God will not condemn people to eternal torment in hell. What they forget is that God is also holy. Sin or filth cannot stain His holiness. He is pure. For everyone to go to Heaven and be with God, they must all be holy, or righteous.

When it's said that "everyone" will go to Heaven, that includes those who don't believe in God and those who have not turned from their sinful life. They haven't accepted the gift that God freely offers them—eternal life through faith in Jesus. These people want to stay mired in the mud and muck of their sins. It's comfortable. It's home for them. They like it. You might say they want to have their cake and eat it too. However, they can't have both at the same time. They can have their cake, but when they eat it, it's gone. They don't have it anymore. Therefore, people can't live in their sin, with no repentance or change, and expect to gain entrance into Heaven. It isn't a both/and situation. It's one or the other.

God is also a righteous judge. If a sinner stays in his sinful life, God will ultimately judge him. The punishment for sin is death (more on this in Chapter 8). God didn't choose this. Each person makes his own choice. My mom helped me understand this.

"Mama, you know how the Holy Spirit fills believers?"

"Well, sure darlin', why?"

"I'm just wondering if the spirit of Satan fills those who don't believe."

"Well, darlin', it's one or the other. Satan or the Holy Spirit."

It's our choice to make. We can either give our lives to Christ or continue living in sin, apart from Jesus. When we choose sin, we separate ourselves forever from God. He doesn't send us to hell. We make the choice: Heaven or hell.

But remember this. God loves us and doesn't want anyone to go to hell. He wants us with Him. He is patiently waiting for us.

"The Lord is not slow about His promise, as some count slowness, but is patient toward you, not wishing for any to perish but for all to come to repentance" (2 Peter 3:9).

Our Lord desires everyone to be saved and to know the truth (1 Timothy 2:4). The original language tells us this is a strong desire of God. It's His will and purpose for us to come to Him. However, God is a gentleman. He gives us the free will to choose. He won't force us to follow Him. The choice is ours. Heaven or hell. It's one or the other. Where will you choose to spend eternity?

Just as we discern Heaven is real, we should also understand that hell is real.

Scripture describes this place. It is called the lake that burns with fire and brimstone (Revelation 21:8). Brimstone is burning sulfur. If you've ever struck a match and an acrid smell reaches your nose, that's sulfur. If you've ever smelled sewer gas or rotten eggs, that is sulfur. And that is hell.

The fire that burns in the lake of hell is eternal (Matthew 25:41, 46). Hell is a place of misery, where there is so much anguish and torment, all you can do is grit your teeth. The fire is a furnace (Matthew 13:42). Have you ever stood next to a fireplace or chiminea to warm up? It feels nice and toasty at first, but the longer you stay there, the hotter it gets. You eventually must move back, so as not to burn your clothes. That's what hell is like. Scorching heat. Fourth-degree burns reach down to a person's bone. And yet, there is no relief.

The punishment for people who choose hell is everlasting destruction (2 Thessalonians 1:9). Everlasting. Lasting forever. Eternal. Pain and suffering forevermore. "The fundamental thought is not annihilation by any means, but unavoidable distress and torment."[1] Unavoidable. You can't get away from it. There is no place to go for even a brief respite. The misery of hell is 24/7. But that's not the worst thing.

Eternal separation from God's presence (2 Thessalonians 1:9) is the most frightful thing about hell. It is a place of darkness (Matthew 8:12). You may wonder how it can be dark, with so much fire. The darkness described is spiritual, because evil and sinfulness dominate hell. There is no light because God is not there. There is weeping and gnashing of teeth. Think of the worst horror movie you saw as a teenager. Do you recall the monster in the movie being in a fit of rage or pain? They grit their rotted teeth, grinding them together. That's gnashing.

Lord, forgive us for not telling others about the right choice!

> *Hell and Heaven are eternal real estate plots. Like real estate, it's all about location, location, location.*

Hell and Heaven are both actual places. They are eternal real estate plots. And just like real estate, it's all about location, location, location. We choose where we want to live for eternity.

Citizens of Heaven

"Honey, can I leave my passport locked in the safe each day while we tour?"

"Absolutely not! We are in a foreign country, and we need our passports with us at all times. They are proof of our identity and that we are in this country legally."

We were on the trip of a lifetime. It was the first time I had ever been overseas! Our church planned a ten-day guided tour through Israel. We were beyond excited to see the Holy Land and walk where Jesus walked.

In a fishing boat, we set out to cruise slowly around the Sea of Galilee, where Jesus instructed Peter to "set out into the deep water." We saw the area where Jesus sent demons into a herd of pigs, and the pigs rushed down a steep bank into the sea. Jesus walked on these very waters!

Of course, there were many stops to make in and around Bethlehem, where Christ was born. The only problem was that Bethlehem was on the west bank. Palestinian territory. Our bus had to stop at checkpoints on the way in and out of that area.

At one checkpoint, a young female soldier boarded our bus and asked to see everyone's passports. We all dutifully pulled them out and held them up, with our pictures showing.

Further behind us, I heard a woman's shrill voice.

"Hani! Hani! We have an issue!" There was panic in every syllable, as this lady called to our tour guide.

Then, sharply "HANI!"

The young soldier continued down the aisle, perusing passports. She didn't notice (or ignored) the frantic passenger. And Hani, our tour guide, never heard the woman's cry for help.

About halfway through, the soldier stopped the intense scrutiny of documents and barely glanced at those in the rear of the bus. This was a good thing because the woman's husband did NOT have his passport. He left it in the hotel safe. Thankfully, he held up his wife's passport, and the soldier didn't give it a second look.

When you are not a citizen of a country, you don't have the rights and privileges of those who live there, those whose home it is.

> ***Heaven is home because we are its citizens.***

Heaven is home because we are its citizens. As citizens, we are people who legally belong to a country and are protected by that country. Citizens adopt the culture and practices of the nation to which they belong.

In his letter to the church at Philippi, Paul explained we are citizens of Heaven (Philippians 3:20). God has His shield of protection around us. As His people, we should adopt the customs and patterns of our Savior, Jesus, and His home (Heaven). Our loyalties lie with Him.

At home in the United States, we have mayors, governors, and a president. But we are first and foremost citizens of Heaven. No matter who our elected officials are, Jesus is still King of our hearts!

Warren Wiersbe says, "D.L. Moody used to scold Christians for being 'so Heavenly minded they were no earthly good,' and that exhortation still needs to be heeded. Christians have a dual citizenship—on earth and in Heaven—and our citizenship in Heaven ought to make us better people here on earth. "[2]

To be better people here on earth, we need to listen to and follow the guidance of the Holy Spirit. Our passport is the Holy Spirit of Jesus, who is always with us. People will notice a difference in us when we follow the Spirit. The fruit of the Holy Spirit will be evident in our lives: love, joy, peace, patience, and kindness, among others. They may even say, "She's not like everyone else. Is she from here? She's different, in a good way!" Always keep your passport close to your heart!

Adopted and Heirs

The second reason Heaven is home is that God, in His love for us, has adopted us. He sent His Son, Jesus, to redeem us. Through Christ's incarnation and death, He secured for believers the full rights of sons. Full rights. God treats us as heirs, not as slaves, or step-children, who have no blood right. Jesus shed His blood to fully draw us into the family of God. As believers in Jesus Christ, we have all the benefits and status of sons and daughters by birth. Because we have been born again (re-birth) we are children of God, adopted by Him.

Paul goes on to say in Romans that if we are heirs, then we are also co-heirs with Christ (Romans 8:17). In New Testament times, adopted sons enjoyed the same privileges as a natural-born son. Warren Wiersbe tells us that "the word adoption in the New Testament means 'being placed as an adult son.' We come into God's family by birth. But the instant we are born into the family, God adopts us and gives us the position of an adult son." [3]

God adopts us and accepts us as His natural-born children.

Just as Jesus is welcome in God's family, as God's Son, so are we. God accepts us. We belong in the family of God as soon as we say yes to His gracious gift of salvation. Being a co-heir with Christ means we will share Jesus' inheritance. Heaven is His home and inheritance. It is ours as well. Since God has made us His children, we have full rights to receive this inheritance.

No lawyers to hire, no legal mumbo jumbo to sort through. We're in!

Our Father's House

"Do you see the houses are many stories high? This is because, as a family grows, each child will make his home on a separate level. The adult child will marry and raise his family in the home of his father. All together, yet separate."

Hani, our tour guide in Israel, explained how Jewish families remained tight-knit. When a son married and started his own family, the groom's father would add rooms onto the top of his house. This tradition began in biblical times and remains today. The families all live under the same roof, yet have separate, private spaces to raise their children.

> *Heaven is our home because it is our Father's house. Jesus is getting our room ready.*

"In My Father's house are many dwelling places; if it were not so, I would have told you; for I go to prepare a place for you. If I go and prepare a place for you, I will come again and receive you to Myself, that where I am, there you may be also" (John 14:2-3).

Heaven is our home because it is our Father's house. Jesus speaks of the many rooms or dwelling places in His Father's house. They are also referred to as mansions. While we may have visions of grand castles, it simply means that we will have living spaces, a room, or a suite (as in the rooms or higher levels added on to the homes of Jewish families).

Jesus is getting this space ready for us. He is preparing our forever home. And then, He will come and take us home with Him. There is a room in the Father's house that is reserved specifically for me, and there is also a room that is meant just for you.

Jesus, the Christ, Lord, and Savior, fixed up our rooms and arranged them for us. Jesus did this. The Savior of the world prepared a home for us that has our name on it. He chose my room because He knows what I need. He knows what I like. Jesus has lovingly selected the furnishings He knows what will fit our personalities. It boggles your brain a bit, doesn't it? I know it does mine. Jesus not only died for me, but He is also making sure I'll have a special place of my own for my homecoming.

This old earth is not our final place. It is temporary. But Jesus promises He's coming back to get us so that we will be with Him (John 14:3). What makes home special is not the things in it, but who is there. And Jesus is waiting for us.

Going Home

"Thank you for your kindness in correcting my meal to kosher. You are doing a wonderful job and are so kind to all!"

My seatmate smiled shyly at the harried flight attendant. It was hard to discern her age because of the hijab she was wearing. But her kind, dark eyes shone bright with love.

It had been a long thirteen-hour flight from Tel Aviv, Israel, to Miami, Florida. During the final two hours, the flight attendants were rushing around, making sure everyone had food. The passengers were waking up, ready to drink coffee before landing. The flight attendants scurried to keep the passengers somewhat happy. It was a hard, thankless job because the passengers were squished together like sardines in a can.

I looked at the kind woman next to me and said, "I do believe you made her day!"

She smiled, and I could see her eyes were young and her face smooth. But there was an age-old sadness about her.

"Do you have family in Miami?"

"No, I will catch another flight and go to Orlando. My mommy is very ill. She had a stroke. I'm going home to see her before…"

Her voice trailed off. Tears stung my eyelids. I nodded, unable to speak. She was going home to see her mommy before her mommy went home.

> *The best part about Heaven being our eternal home is being with Jesus. Forever. The next best thing is being reunited with our loved ones.*

Home is where your heart is. This young woman's heart was with her mom. There is no place like home with your loved ones. The best part about Heaven being our eternal home is being with Jesus. Forever. The next best thing is being reunited with our loved ones.

Our trip was a dream come true, but it was long. There's a lot to be said for sleeping in your own bed, on your own pillow. Walking into the door of our home, I felt like Dorothy in the Wizard of Oz. There's no place like home! There's no place like home!

Unpacking and piddling around the house, I could feel the tension rolling off my shoulders after hours of travel. I felt safe again. Home is my safe place.

Finally, I took a minute to sit down and exhale. Then promptly burst into tears.

It hit me like a ton of bricks. The rest I was feeling, the release of tension, the safety of my home—this is what Mama must have felt when she entered the gates of Heaven. She was home, her eternal safe place.

"Finally home!" I imagine she said, as she walked through the gates of pearls on the golden streets of Heaven.

That's why she smiled.

• • • • • • • • • •

Stepping Stone #7

RECOGNIZE:
Heaven is home for all those who place their faith in Jesus.

REFLECT on God's Word:
2 Peter 3:9

Philippians 3:20

RESPOND to the questions:

- Do you believe hell is real? Why or why not? What led you to this belief?

- You are a co-heir with Jesus Christ. How do you feel about that—worthy or unworthy? Journal about why you feel this way.

- What do you imagine your living space will be like in Heaven?

Chapter 8

WHY DO WE BELONG IN HEAVEN?

*For the Christian, Heaven is where Jesus is. We do not need to
speculate on what Heaven will be like. It will be enough to know
that we will be forever with Him.*
~William Barclay

IT WAS CHAOS. ORGANIZED and fun, but still chaos. Kids were
everywhere. Seven years up to seventeen, they had taken over my
house and yard. It was enough to make this empty nester's eye twitch
with nerves.

My husband and I were having a party for the children our church
hosted each summer. They came from the country of Belarus to
spend six weeks in the United States for fresh air and clean food.
Roughly two-thirds of their country became contaminated because
of the radioactive fallout from the Chernobyl power plant disaster.
Our church housed several children each summer, feeding them,
loving them, and telling them about Jesus.

I was out of my element, never having birthed a baby of my own.
And I like my house neat and orderly. That day, however, it was a
crazy mess. There was food everywhere (even in places it shouldn't

be). Wet swimsuits left puddles all over my wood floors. Sticky hand-shaped smears marred the clear glass of my patio doors. I took it all in stride, loving the hugs of the children, and the many "Sank you, Miss Ellen. Sank you!"

Messy house, sloppy kids. Not my thing. And yet, my heart was singing. I've never felt more alive. This is where I belonged.

That's how God feels about us. Messy, sloppy, and imperfect as we are, God created us to be with Him. But our sin separates us from God.

When sin entered the picture, man went from innocent obedience to sinful disobedience. But God! He knew this would happen, and He had a plan for eternal salvation. We can see this in the metanarrative of scripture, which is the overarching theme or story that gives meaning to all the smaller stories in the Bible. In short, the metanarrative of scripture is Creation, Fall, Redemption, and Restoration.

God created the world and each of us. He knew humans would sin (fall short of His standard), so He sent Jesus to redeem us from sin and death. Jesus' death on the cross is God's gift to us. It restores us to Him. Jesus died to save us. Those who have accepted this wonderful, gracious gift will have eternal life and belong in Heaven with Jesus.

Complete restoration will come when we are fully and finally restored to God at Christ's return.

God's ways are higher than our ways. His plan is perfect, even when we think our plans are better. He knows all things and has a purpose for us. He wants us to be with Him. Heaven is our inheritance, and it is God's original plan. Let's look and see, directly from God, why we belong in Heaven.

Because of Jesus

When we surrender our lives to Christ, we are united with Him. Scripture clearly tells us we belong to Christ (1 Corinthians 3:23). The common phrase for this is being "in Christ." Jesus' blood brings those who are in Christ near to God (Ephesians 2:13). Paul tells the church in Rome that if anyone does not have the Spirit of Christ, they don't belong to Him (Romans 8:9). At the moment we give our lives to Christ, His Holy Spirit enters us. Therefore, we belong to Jesus.

Taking a childlike step of faith and asking Jesus to be Lord and Savior of our lives, means we will—to the best of our ability—commit to live our lives for Him. It's a big change. We are new creations because of Jesus. We become a member of the body of Christ (the Church).

Because Jesus is sitting at the right hand of His Father in Heaven, and because we belong to Him, we belong in Heaven with Him. It's as simple as that.

We belong in Heaven because Jesus saved us.

From what are we saved? The Bible tells us it is sin and death.

Everyone is born into this world a sinner (Romans 3:23). Yes, even that cute grandbaby of yours with the precious rolls of fat around his knees and the drool dripping from his grinning, toothless mouth. He's nothing but a little sinner.

I know what you're thinking, "Not MY precious grandchild!" Yes, yours. And mine.

Why?

It's our sinful nature. We are born with the desire to do as we please, not as God pleases. We are wired to do what is right in our own eyes.

Think of your sweet grandchild when he reaches the age of, oh, let's say, the terrible twos. What are his favorite words?

"No!"

"Mine!"

He wants what he wants when he wants it. Mankind is inherently selfish. That is the sin nature in all of us—we want what we want, and not what God wants for us. Disobedience, rebellion, not following God's laws, and lack of faith are signs of sin in our lives. Sin separates us from our holy God. Scripture says the penalty for sin is death (Romans 6:23). This is a spiritual death—eternal separation from God in Heaven. Our choice is Heaven with God or an eternity in hell without Him.

But there is good news! God sent Jesus to pay our penalty (Romans 5:8). Imagine yourself convicted of a heinous crime. You stand before the judge waiting for sentencing, knowing full well you did what the prosecution alleged. Your heart flutters and there is a sheen of perspiration on your upper lip.

"Guilty!" the judge declares. "The court deems that you shall die by lethal injection." Your knees are knocking. You stumble, almost falling to the ground. Your last hope just went up in flames.

At that instant, a gentleman walks up and stands beside you.

"Judge, I'd like to take the penalty for this person. I will die in her place."

"That's very unusual, sir! May I ask your name and why you would do this?"

"My name is Jesus. I'm doing this because I love her and want her to be with Me in Heaven."

"Ma'am, do you accept this generous gift from this Man?"

"Yes! Oh, yes, your honor, I do!"

Jesus had no sin in Him, but He took our sins on His shoulders. He was born to die so that—even though we face certain death—we will live forever. Jesus died the death we deserve. He was broken for our brokenness so that we can be made whole in Him (1 Corinthians 11:24).

Think about this: He didn't just die for me; He died as me. But the best news? He rose again to a new life. We will too!

God wants us to be with Him. And Jesus does too! It's hard to comprehend, isn't it? Our focus is on the here and now. We immerse ourselves in the things of the world while Jesus patiently waits for us.

Jesus tells the Father that He desires us to be with Him (John 17:24). The original Greek for "desire" means "to wish, desire, choose."[1]

> *When we walk through Heaven's gate, Jesus will greet us.*

Jesus' wish is for us to be where He is. That's His choice and His will. It's what He longs for. And, since He knows each of us by name when we walk through Heaven's gate, Jesus will greet us. He'll be excited to see us!

"Ellen! I've been waiting! You're home! I'm so excited you are here!" In my mind's eye, I can see Jesus jumping up and down, clapping His nail-scarred hands.

We shed many tears at Mama's funeral and other funerals. But here's what God's Word says about the death of one of His own:

"Precious in the sight of the Lord is the death of His godly ones" (Psalm 116:15).

Oh, how we grieved when Mama died. But Jesus. He was looking forward to her arrival in Heaven. He was thrilled to see her and welcomed her with great rejoicing!

"Miss Ann, welcome home! I've got your room ready!"

Because it's God's Original Plan

In the beginning.

This is where we see God's original plan.

In Genesis, we find the beautiful story of God's creation. He created everything we would need to live—air, sky, earth, water, plants, and animals. After that, He created humans. We meet them in the pages of scripture and see the plan He has for them. God created man (and woman) in His image. Eden, a lush garden, is where God placed the man Adam and his wife Eve. There was no shortage of food because God had created every living plant needed for sustenance.

God created man to be in fellowship with Him. God, along with Adam and Eve, walked in the garden together during the cool of the day (Genesis 3:8). Can you picture the peace that filled Adam and Eve? A lovely natural home, with fresh food all the time. And the best part? Walking closely with God. Being in His presence. God designed us to walk in perfect harmony with Him.

Until that scoundrel, the devil, caused Adam and Eve to be discontent with what they had. And believe me, they had it all! Adam and Eve disobeyed God, sinning against Him. It's been a vicious cycle since. Rebellion, repentance, redemption, restoration. Over and over.

But one day, it will end.

Eden is gone, but there is something far better coming. A new garden. A better garden. On the Main Street in New Jerusalem.

There is a river flowing through the new garden, from the throne of God and Jesus, down the middle of the street of gold. This water is pure and clear as crystal. It is life-giving water. The tree of life is on either side of the river.

Scripture doesn't provide many details about this garden. However, it wouldn't be a stretch to envision winding, tree-shaded paths meandering through it. The river may culminate in a waterfall that will take your breath away. When brilliant light from the Son shines down on the cascading water, a rainbow forms. It is a beautiful reminder of God's promise that He will never again destroy the earth by flood (Genesis 9:13).

The tree of life will provide twelve varieties of fruit. There is fruit each month. An assortment of plants and flowers abound in the new garden. The plants will bear vegetables for sustenance, and the flowers will delight the senses—multi-colored petals, like a patchwork quilt, and the delightful smells of lilac, sweet olive, and rose to tease your nose.

This earth began with a garden, and a garden will end this earth as we know it. Eden is gone, but it will be re-birthed "in a City that is like a garden paradise."[2]

The apostle John saw this new holy city coming down out of Heaven. He called it the New Jerusalem (Revelation 21:10-14). He also saw the new Heaven and earth coming down out of Heaven (Revelation 21:1). The city has a high wall with twelve gates. Each gate has a name representing the twelve tribes of the sons of Israel. The wall of the city has twelve foundation stones.

Many commentaries have described the area of the city as being a square, with height, length, and width of about 1,400 miles each. It will be vast. You can see the foundation stones at the base of the city wall. These stones speak to the permanence of the city. Compare this to Abraham's tents, where sojourners and strangers lived in temporary housing (Hebrews 11:8-10).

Beautiful jewels adorn the walls of the city. Pearls cover the city gates. However, the jewels don't represent opulence. Jen Wilkin has this to say about it:

> "The New Jerusalem is a first-is-last place, where the things we have exalted will be cast down to the level of their real worth: as mere metal and stone...It is a place where precious metals and stones are trodden under foot as common road dust...where the people and objects and institutions to which we have ascribed our worship will fall from their lofty places. It is a place whose inhabitants at last obey the first word: 'You shall have no other gods before me.' It is Eden restored."[3]

We belong in Heaven because it is God's original plan to be with His people. Forever.

The "things" we consider precious—wealth, status, outward appearances—will mean nothing to us in Heaven. Once we are home, we will never focus on "things" again. Why? Because the most beautiful and fulfilling thing about this new city is that God and Jesus are there with us. There is no need for the sun to shine because the Son provides light.

We belong in Heaven because it is God's original plan to be with His people. Forever.

What About When the Earth Burns Up? What Happens Then?

The apostle Peter also describes the new Heaven and earth.

"But the day of the Lord will come like a thief, in which the Heavens will pass away with a roar and the elements will be destroyed with intense heat, and the earth and its works will be burned up... But according to His promise we are looking for new Heavens and a new earth, in which righteousness dwells" (2 Peter 3:10, 13).

How does the earth burning up fit in with the new Heaven and new earth? To me, it's kind of like sugar cane harvest.

A funny thing happens in South Louisiana in the fall. The sugar mills rumble and roar. They spew out white smoke that smells like burned sugar on a good day and dog poop on a bad day. Harvest season has begun.

After harvesting the cane from the fields, farmers burn off excess cane leaves and stalks. Consumed by the fire that clears the chaff and waste, they turn into heaps of ashes. The fields lay bare and burned. Rows and rows of blackened, fallen stalks scream, "No hope! No hope!" Flames destroyed them, leaving no expectation of life or usefulness again. The ashes mark the end of the harvest.

Ah, but in a day or two, tiny shoots of green sprout up, ready to grow sweet cane for next season's harvest.

How can that be? There is nothing left of the sugar cane except ashes. But deep in the ground, below the topsoil, a root ball survived.

The roots are still alive and growing, watered by the condensation from the heat above. They are a remnant of the former grand stalks of cane. From the remains, new cane sprouts and brings hope of an abundant harvest.

> *God said He would make all things new, not all new things.*

That remnant—the root ball—is the beginning of the new earth. God said He would make all things new, not all new things (Revelation 21:5). When Peter tells us the earth will burn up, he is talking about judgment. God exposes all the evil works, laying them bare and burning them up. The fire burns all the bad and useless, so the good can flourish, grow, and prosper. The new earth remains. "God seems always to renew, not destroy and recreate, parts of his creation that are marred by sin."[4]

All things new, not all new things. As it should be.

Why?

Because God wouldn't trash something He created and considered good (Genesis 1).

Because We Get to Spend Eternity with Jesus

The new earth is Heaven. It is the hope of home that we have been longing for. It is the better place Abraham was seeking. We'll have the better identity Daniel knew. We won't long for "what was" like the returning exiles did because we will be with Jesus.

The one thing that fills all the longings of our hearts is Jesus. He is the answer to our heart's ache. Jesus is the answer to all we desire. With Him, our lives are full. There is no lack when Jesus is our treasure (Luke 22:35, 1 Corinthians 1:7).

> *Jesus fills all the longings of our hearts.*

Warren Wiersbe says that Heaven is more than a destination; it is a motivation.[5] For months after my mom passed away, I missed her terribly. It was a physical ache in my heart. I wanted more than anything to hear her voice again. I longed for Heaven because I knew she was there.

Now, I know much more. I still miss my Mama. But what I've found is far better: my real home. I long for Heaven, because I know it's real, I know it's home, and I know without a doubt it's where I belong.

We won't just spend eternity in Heaven. We will spend it with Jesus.

Long for Him.

But I'm Still Homesick

But why am I still homesick?

It's because we are living the "Yes, but not yet." We are members of God's kingdom. Christ is in us, the hope of glory. We possess His Holy Spirit as a down payment for what is coming. But we must patiently wait for Jesus to return and take us home with Him. No one knows when that time will be. Yes, He's coming, but not yet.

Yes, His kingdom is glorious. But we won't see the full glory of God's kingdom until we are home with Him.

C.S. Lewis said this: "If you read history you will find that the Christians who did most for the present world were just those who thought most of the next."[6] Yes, we're homesick now for the new Heavens and earth. While we wait for all things to be made new, we can live in the now, anticipating the future with great hope.

It's like reading an excellent novel. There is tension until the story resolves. This is called denouement, which is the final part of a story when everything is explained. Living in the tension of the "not yet" is much the same. Our denouement comes when we are finally home. That's when there is resolution, and we find ourselves redeemed and restored.

The Old Testament saints (Enoch, Abraham, Sarah, Noah) all died believing in the promises of God. They haven't yet received those promises (Hebrews 11:13). They all followed God based on the hope of a future homeland, a better identity, a more glorious future, and a better home. The same is true for us. God's future kingdom, our eternal home, is our hope. We are already a part of this kingdom spiritually, but physically we remain here on earth.

How do we daily live in the "Yes, but not yet?" We endure the now and keep our eyes on the day Jesus comes. We rejoice! Even when we don't feel like it. Even when we don't have what we are waiting for.

Wait patiently. God is faithful. The kingdom of Heaven is at hand!

Our lives on earth are a journey. We are strangers, sojourners, and pilgrims headed home. We are exiles, longing for home. With each step we take toward home, we rejoice in our identity: Exiles for Christ, longing to be with Him.

• • • ● • ● • • •

Stepping Stone #8

RECOGNIZE:
We belong in Heaven because it's God's original plan.

REFLECT on God's Word:
John 17:24
2 Peter 3:10, 13

RESPOND to the questions:
- Do you believe Jesus fills every longing of your heart? What worldly things do you reach for to fill you? Does it work?

- Are you as excited to see Jesus one day as He is to see and welcome you home? What's the first thing you might say to Him?

- List three things you can do to live with great anticipation of the new Heaven and earth (example: memorize scriptures about Heaven, etc).

Part 3

· · · · · · ● · · · · · ·

On Our Journey Home

We

Rejoice as Exiles

Chapter 9

REJOICING AS EXILES

Hold loosely to the things of this life, so that if God requires them of you, it will be easy to let them go.
~Corrie Ten Boom

"IT'S HARD TO THINK of eternity," she said, brow furrowed. The discussion in our Bible study led to talk about Heaven. Many of the young-ish couples agreed with her.

"I mean, it's like *forever*. How do you wrap your brain around that?"

Indeed, how do we? How do we move from a temporal mindset to an eternal one?

I struggled with this very problem after my mom died. My mom was home in Heaven. So I started learning about her new home. However, I struggled to change my thinking to this higher level. I was stuck on the events and problems at hand, right in front of me. My home is the three-bedroom, two-bath structure the Lord had blessed us with, not the glorious forever home I had been learning about.

Something needs to change. And it needs to be me.

Do you know the definition of insanity? It's doing the same thing, over and over and over, and expecting different results. A beautiful cardinal showed me how this works.

He showed up at my office window one day. The office is nestled among beautiful rolling hills, with a bayou meandering through the property. The wooded acreage brought a variety of wildlife parading in front of my window. Deer, rabbits, bobcats, and yes, even snakes would make appearances. There was a massive assortment of birds. Ducks, anhingas, and egrets, along with bluebirds and cardinals, brought color and life to my work days. It was lovely. Until it wasn't.

The bright crimson cardinal perched on the windowsill, gazing at me quizzically. Then he flew off. Seconds later "BAM!" That kamikaze bird flew right into the window. I thought he must have knocked his bird brain out, but he flew away. And then came right back! Bam!

Over and over, that lunatic cardinal flew into my office window. I assume he thought he could get inside. Instead, he just knocked his head against the window. Over and over. For months! He did this every day. Insanity!!

Just like me. Just like the way I've been thinking about eternity. The same old, same old, never changing what I thought about it. It was just something that lasted forever.

I knew I needed to change the way I thought about Heaven and my eternal home. But how?

Brain Ruts

As it turns out, your brain gets into a groove in the way it thinks. Having the same thought over and over makes "ruts" in your brain.

The more you have the thought, the deeper the rut or trench.[1] These trenches are called neural pathways.

In simple terms, a brain rut is like a well-worn path. The first time you travel that way, there may be tall weeds. You can't see the path. But as you traverse it day by day, you trample the weeds and hard-packed earth remains.

Our brains automate our behaviors, beating down the "weeds." Brushing your teeth, for instance. You don't have to think through each step to brush your teeth: take the cap off the toothpaste, put paste on the toothbrush, brush, spit, rinse, dry, and put away the toothbrush. Your brain sends a message along the neural pathway telling you what action to take. When it is a frequently traveled path (as in a habit), the neural pathway becomes well-worn. The more we do something or think a certain way, the deeper and more hard-packed the neural pathway becomes.

Our brains take the path of least resistance. This is good news and bad news. The good news is we don't have to remember to do the simplest things. However, when the rut is deep, it's harder to change our behavior or pattern of thinking.

When we repeat the phrase "I can't, I can't, I can't" it becomes a struggle to believe we *can*. When we say "It's hard to think about eternity" then, yes, it is hard. The more we think these thoughts, the deeper our brain ruts. It's hard to climb out of a deep gully.

But the good news is, we can retrain our brains. For the secular world, those who don't believe in Jesus, I would argue that it's a hard thing to do. Non-Christians struggle to make changes because they work in their own strength. But Christians? We are new creations in Christ Jesus. We have the power of the Holy Spirit in us to renew our minds (Romans 12:1-2).

It seems impossible, doesn't it? To change a habit or thought pattern. Historically, home has been a physical structure where families, pets, and neighbors live. How do we make "new ruts?"

By filling our thoughts with truth. How we think is how we will live. And we need to live as exiles, pondering our heavenly home. When we read and study what God says about Heaven and eternity, our brains will know the truth and make new ruts.

It starts with letting go, looking up, and learning to live as exiles.

Let Go and Loosen Up

We hold so many things with a death grip. Grudges, for instance. Unforgiveness is the first thing we need to let go of when we open our hands.

Oh my. Let go of my hurt and anger? Let the person who harmed me just run free to hurt someone else? How in the world can I do that?

We can't, in our worldly selves. We need to pray for the power of the Holy Spirit to enable us to have a forgiving heart.

Yes, us. Not the one who hurt us. Forgiveness begins in our hearts. How can you pray to forgive that person? Ask the Holy Spirit to help you forgive with His power and His gracious love. Seek His strength to soften your heart and supernaturally allow you to forgive.

God is our ultimate reconciler. He gave us Jesus to reconcile us to Himself. How much more would He want us reconciled to others?

Forgive without keeping count.

Remember when Peter asked Jesus how often he must forgive a brother who continues to sin against him (Matthew 18:21-22)? He thought seven was a generous amount, since in Judaism three times was enough to show a forgiving spirit. But Jesus. He calls us to more. He told Peter that seventy times seven was sufficient. Now, don't be like me and do the math. What Jesus is talking about is forgiving without keeping count. We forgive by deciding not to hold on to our anger or grudge, no matter what the other person has done. This is what a true disciple would do. This is how exiles strive to live.

Seven is also a biblical number of completion. When we forgive others of offenses, the issue is complete. We no longer need to bring it up constantly in conversations or let it consume our thoughts. Over. Done. Complete.

What happens when the tables are turned? When we are the one who has wronged another? What if this person won't forgive us, even when we've apologized and tried to reconcile? Let kindness flow through your actions, thoughts, and words. Bear with one another and forgive (Ephesians 4:32, Colossians 3:13). Why? Because the Lord has forgiven us.

Above all, live in harmony with others, do not repay evil for evil, and "If possible, so far as it depends on you, be at peace with all men" (Romans 12:18).

> *Life is too short to carry the burden of unforgiven hurts and unresolved conflicts.*

Life is too short to carry the burden of unforgiven hurts and unresolved conflicts. Trust that God will judge. Let it go!

Letting go of something huge, like a long-standing grudge, will make it easier to let go of stuff. Things. All the tangibles we cling to.

My first Christmas without Mama taught me about letting go and holding things loosely.

I dreaded that first Christmas without her. My heart was heavy at the thought of it. Not that I was always at my mom's house for Christmas. Not that she was at my home for the holidays. But she was always *there*. And now she's not. Grief filled me during the first Christmas season without her.

I love all things Christmas. Love, *love*, **love.** Decorating the house and putting up the tree make me clap my hands in joy. I love the lights, the holly, and the red berries. But not that year.

I tried to convince myself that being out among Christmas things would make me feel joyful.

"Maybe if I go shopping and 'refresh' some of my decorations, I'll perk up. Maybe my mood will lighten." Off I went, ready for new stuff!

{Sigh.}

I left the store that day with a car full of holly and red berries, and an empty heart. It was just as empty and sorrowful as it was before my shopping spree. I cried all the way home. "What is Christmas like in Heaven?" I wondered. The realization struck me: all my glitz and glitter is nothing compared to being with Jesus on His birthday! And Mama is there with Him. She will love it!

"Things" couldn't fill the emptiness in my heart. Even things that normally make me happy.

The only way to fill my heart was to empty my hands. I learned to hold the temporary things of this world with open hands. It was a hard-fought battle to change the way I think. I love my things. God has blessed me with an abundance. Of stuff. Wonderful stuff like a home, a car, a job (and then retirement). But it's all temporary. One day I'll be home in glory and my stuff will rot and decay.

Warren Wiersbe and Charles Spurgeon have great wisdom about letting go.

Wiersbe says, "What does it mean to lay up treasures in Heaven? It means to use all that we have for the glory of God. It means to 'hang loose' when it comes to the material things of life."[2]

Spurgeon adds this to our wisdom: "Hold everything earthly with a loose hand; but grasp eternal things with a death-like grip."[3] This is the exact opposite of what we naturally do.

Why, then, do we feel the need for "things" to fill us and supposedly satisfy us? We can't seem to resist the more visible, bright, shining object to fill our needs. In her book, ***The Promise is His Presence***, Glenna Marshall says:

> "It's easier to quiet our longings with physical things that bring immediate, quantifiable relief...God has always been enough for His people, but we've always been on the lookout for something more—even though seeking satisfaction in anything "more" than God's full presence will unquestionably lead to less."[4]

Jesus is Immanuel, God with us. As believers, we have His Holy Spirit in us always. His presence is always with us and fills us. In His presence we find our joy (Psalm 16:11). God commands us to seek His presence and set our minds on Jesus. It takes practice. When we acknowledge His presence time after time, our brain will re-train itself to know instinctively He is always with us.

Recently, my husband went to a men's retreat and was gone overnight. While I wasn't lonely or scared, I missed his presence. It is comfortable and comforting, steady and steadying, solid and safe. When he's home, even when there is little conversation, I know he's here. His presence speaks to me. I feel his love.

> *Jesus' presence is comfortable and comforting, steady and steadying, solid and safe.*

That is what it's like to have Jesus' presence with us always. Staring intently above us, we see Jesus in all His glory. And we know His presence is all we need.

By holding things loosely, we look to Jesus to fill us. Nothing can compare to that!

Look Up

During the season of loss after Mama went to Heaven, the burden of grief was overwhelming. So John and I left. We took off. We weren't running away from our problems, exactly. But we believed a change of scenery was necessary. We wanted to be steeped in nature and feel God's presence in His creation. So we ran.

Oh, not from the grief. It would follow us and eventually work its way through us. But in order to exhale, we took a vacation. There was scenery we had never laid eyes on and we wanted to explore and photograph. Our minds and bodies longed to retreat and rest in the arms of our Creator.

Out west we saw sweeping vistas atop flat terra cotta mesas. Discovering Mesa Verde, which housed the remains of the Cliff Dwellers, awed us. These people built their homes and villages on the side of stone cliffs. We easily made our way down the cliff by clutching the guard rail and following winding steps carved into stone.

Getting out was a different story. There was a primitive wooden ladder in a narrow confined space we had to climb. The space was like a slot between two enormous boulders. It was probably three or four feet wide but seemed so much smaller when you gazed at it from the bottom.

John took one look at me and said, "You won't make it, will you?" He knew my fear of tight spaces—those little enclosed areas that make breathing difficult.

Watching the person in front of me climb the rungs of the rickety ladder, my anxiety ticked up a notch. He was, um, well, a big guy! When he went up through the slot, there was no sky to be seen above him. A complete blackout. If I followed too closely, and he got stuck, I'm pretty sure I would hyperventilate!

So I waited and waited, and waited some more, until he crawled out. The second I could see daylight, I hopped on that old creaky ladder and climbed as fast as I could to the top.

Keeping my focus on the blue sky above, I didn't look right or left at the walls of thick stone. My eyes and my mind focused on what was above. Just like scripture taught me.

Keep seeking and set your mind on the things above (Colossians 3:1-2). What's above? Heaven and Christ, who is sitting next to God.

Scripture commands us to keep seeking things above. Don't stop desiring the things above. Have a heavenly mindset always.

How? Again, it's our brain. We set our minds on things above. The more we think about Heaven and all its benefits, the more it will become our natural default. God created us with these marvelous brains to help us think of Him. And with His supernatural enabling, we can renew our minds and the way we think.

Often, we struggle with the eternal when we are smack dab in the middle of the immediate. So many things vie for our attention that it's hard to focus on something we can't see. We rush through our days, panic rising at every minor catastrophe that comes our way. When I have days like this, I'm a basket case by evening. How about you?

But when we refocus and seek the things above, our brains will have a reboot. We realize that these mini-disasters don't need us in emergency mode. God is in control. We need only to look to Him. And pray. A lot!

Instead of focusing on our earthly treasures, we seek treasures in Heaven. Where our treasure is, our hearts will also be (Matthew 6:21).

Treasure in Heaven

Why are our lives so earthbound? We measure our success by what we have accomplished and how much stuff we have. People perceive us as more successful when we have more stuff. But it isn't about quantity. It's about quality. It isn't how much we have, but how long our treasures will last. Are our treasures temporary or eternal?

How do we store up treasures in Heaven? Scripture compares treasures on earth to those in Heaven. Earthly treasures are temporary. My car will age and have to be replaced. One day, my house will be so old and run down that no amount of maintenance will save it.

The trees and flowers I plant have a limited life span. Why, even my body, which I'm taking care of by watching what I eat and exercising, will wear out, die, and decay. All my worldly possessions will turn to dust.

Our earthly treasures are material things that don't last. We can become slaves to them. I like my home, but I would love to have a bigger, better version with more property. If I get that, I'll be shackled to that big old house because of the care and constant maintenance.

Without realizing it, our earthly treasures can eventually dominate our lives. Worse still, they won't last. Treasures built on earth "are subject to decay (moth destroys cloth and rust destroys metal; cf. James 5:2–3) or theft, whereas treasures deposited in Heaven can never be lost."[5] Everything God does will last forever. Destruction awaits all of man's works and strivings.

Heavenly treasures are eternal. There is no destroying them. We can store up these eternal treasures by knowing God. We can know Him through His Word. By knowing our heavenly Father and His Son, we will grow our relationship with Him. This is where we find genuine joy. Not in the things of this world, but living in a close relationship with Jesus.

We also store eternal treasures when we grow God's kingdom. Using our time and money (treasures) to build the Church are wise investments in eternity. Now, I'm not just talking about the brick and mortar building. I'm speaking of the people that comprise the Church. Making disciples is an eternal endeavor. Matter of fact, Jesus commanded it. "Go therefore and make disciples"(Matthew 28:19). When we actively build and grow God's Church, we are storing treasures in Heaven. Sharing the good news about Jesus and winning souls for Him are treasures without end. Eternal, never to decay.

Who Are Exiles?

Storing up treasures in Heaven and seeking the things above will soon have us thinking like exiles.

Why exiles? Because that is who we are.

The book of 2 Kings tells of the exiles being taken to Babylon. They were the royalty, the best of the best. They were the cream of the crop: craftsmen, nobility, and mighty men of valor (2 Kings 24:14). Only the poorest of the poor remained in Jerusalem.

Exiles are the best of the best for God. That is who we should be while we are here on this earth. An exile lives in a forced absence from their country or home. We are in that state now, as we (those of us still living on earth) can't be home with God and Jesus until the rapture or we die.

Remember Abraham? Abe was called by God to leave his home in Ur. He was an exile. Yet he earnestly desired a new country, a heavenly one. A home where he wouldn't be a stranger.

And Daniel! Exiled in Babylon from his homeland, he had confidence in his identity with God. He prayed for his homeland. Ultimately, he looked forward to the day he would receive his new identity.

The returning exiles in the book of Ezra are God's people coming home. They longed for the beauty and glory of the temple that was destroyed. Eventually, they understood God's plans for their better future.

Paul visited Heaven and then returned to earth. He recognized Heaven as home. For a time, he was an exile here on earth. Like me. Like you.

Who are the exiles? We are. Heaven is our eternal homeland. We are exiles on earth waiting to go home. While we are here, we should be the best of the best for our Savior. We should bring a little of the peace, love, and joy of our heavenly homeland to earth with us, sharing it with others.

In the New Testament, Peter calls the exiles "chosen" and God's "elect" (1 Peter 1:1). We are God's chosen people to represent Him to a lost and dying world. How then should we live while we are here on earth?

Rejoice!

Let's rejoice and embrace our identities as exiles. To rejoice as exiles is to know we are in exile for our Savior Jesus. We are His best people, chosen to represent Him while we are away from our heavenly home.

> *When we cultivate a heavenly mindset, we are rejoicing as exiles.*

When we cultivate a heavenly mindset, we are rejoicing as exiles. With joy, we open our hands and our hearts and grab hold of eternity. We loosen up and let go of worldly things.

We begin our rejoicing with faith and confidence as we long for our eternal home.

• • • ● • ● ● • • •

Stepping Stone #9

REJOICE:
You are an exile with a heavenly mindset.

REFLECT on God's Word:
Romans 12:1-2
Matthew 6:21

RESPOND to the questions:

- What heavenly concepts might you meditate on to rewire your brain? How can you carve out some time to meditate on the eternal?

- Is there someone you've been unable to forgive? A hurt that you can't forget? Write a prayer asking God to give you His strength to forgive, and let go of the hurt.

- Fill in the blank: Life's too short, but it's never too late to
_____ .

Chapter 10

REJOICING IN FAITH

You will not be carried to Heaven lying at ease upon a feather bed.

  ~Samuel Rutherford

FEAR GRIPPED THEM, SNAKING its way around their hearts. Terror squeezed every bit of courage out of them. God told them He would part the waters of the Jordan River so they could cross over. The memory of walking across the dried Red Sea still amazed them. God had dried it until there were cracks in the mud! There was no water left where they crossed over. But crossing through the Jordan? This was different.

The Jordan was overflowing its banks. Spring rains and melting snow from Mount Hermon caused the usually placid river to become swollen. The rushing waters threatened the safety of the Israelites with their power. This was not normal! Typically three to ten feet deep, the waters were much deeper now. The floods had caused the river to swell to over 100 feet wide.

Because of a famine, they left their homeland over 400 years ago. Now, almost home, they were exiles no more. Crossing the dangerously swollen river was the last leg of their journey.

Along with the flooding, the priests who carried the Ark of the Covenant had to put their feet in the swiftly moving waters first (Joshua 3). They didn't have to do this at the Red Sea crossing. But now? Before God would part the waters, the priests had to be obedient and step into the water. What if the waters swept them away?

With much trembling and trepidation, the priests let their feet touch the water. Immediately, they saw it: The swollen waters of the Jordan rose and stood, like a great wall (Joshua 3:16).

The priests walked to the middle of the Jordan and stood on dry ground. They remained there until all Israel had passed through. The faith they had in God gave them the strength to touch the raging waters. They believed God would do what He said: dry up the swollen river, so they would have safe passage across.

Oh, how they must have rejoiced when they reached the other side! After all, for exiles heading home, there is much to rejoice over. They had overcome their fear of crossing the swollen flood waters.

How were they able to get over their great fear?

With greater faith.

What is faith?

Faith is trusting in something you can't see or can't prove to be true, according to Hebrews 11:1. The Israelites couldn't prove that God would dry up the Jordan. But they trusted Him. They had seen Him act on their behalf at the Red Sea, and they believed He would provide for them again just as He had in the forty years in between.

Our faith is in our mighty God and His Son Jesus. We believe Jesus paid the price for our sins by His death on the cross. He died to defeat death and Satan, and He rose again to give us the hope of eternal life. We trust Jesus will keep us and bring us home to Him one day.

Faith does wonderful things for us. Our faith in Jesus justifies us. Justification is when God declares that sinners who believe in Jesus are righteous. It is an act by God, "and not a process...Since we are justified by faith, it is an instant and immediate transaction between the believing sinner and God. If we were justified by works, then it would have to be a gradual process."[1]

Living by faith frees us from fear. When we walk by faith in Jesus, we know He holds us in His hands. We have no reason to fear, because He is with us. Faith freed the Israelites at the Jordan River because it became greater than their fear.

Growing Faith

How did the Israelites attain this great faith?

By knowing God.

Mary DeMuth says it this way. "Faith is based on relationship. If you struggle to trust God, it simply means you have more to know about Him because to know Him is to believe His good intentions toward us."[2]

The Israelites knew God because He rescued them from Pharoah. The Lord brought them out of Egypt and delivered them. He provided for them in their exodus. Through Moses, God instructed the Israelites to take articles of silver and gold from the Egyptians (Exodus 3:22, 12:25-36). Not only that, the Egyptians were glad when they left (Psalm 105:37-38)! I can just hear them now: *Buh bye! Go on now, git!*

The Hebrews spent time with God in the wilderness. For forty years, they walked closely with Him. He guided them in a cloud by day and in a fire by night. God fed them manna from Heaven. Their clothes never wore out (Deuteronomy 8:4). God cared for His children.

Because they had lived in Egypt for so long, many did not know Him at the beginning of their journey. During those forty years of wandering in the desert, God taught them about Himself. He showed them His love for them. Thus, the wilderness years gave the Israelites a history with God.

He wants us to have a history with Him, too. God wants us to learn about Him and His Son Jesus. He wants to teach us about His love for us. He shares this love through His Word, the Holy Bible. God will teach us as we read and study the scriptures. And—as my pastor says—when we read scriptures we are hearing from Heaven!

Like the Israelites, when we learn about God and know Him, our faith will grow. There is an indelible mark He leaves on our lives. We'll be able to look back and say, "See what God has done!"

Knowing God and experiencing Him will grow our faith exponentially from its mustard seed beginnings. Jesus tells us in one of His parables that if we have faith the size of a mustard seed, we can move mountains (Matthew 17:20).

Have you ever examined a mustard seed? They are very tiny, smaller than a BB. One day, I took a seed out of the spice jar. Who knows why I had whole mustard seeds? Probably an obscure recipe I never made. Anyway, I read the scripture in Matthew and wanted to see what the mustard seed was like.

Again, it is small. But let me tell you, that little mustard seed was hard on the outside. I tried to break it. With a hammer. I couldn't crush it.

Mustard seed faith is strong, rock-solid faith. And it is a growing faith. From the tiny mustard seed, a tree can grow an average of twenty feet tall, with the width of its branches growing the same. Jesus said the mustard seed was smaller than all other seeds. But watch out! When it's full grown, it is larger than other garden plants and becomes a tree (Matthew 13:31-32).

> *Mustard seed faith is strong, rock-solid faith.*

How do we move from having little faith to having strong faith? As exiles, we grow our faith by knowing God through His Word and doing what it says. One obedient step at a time.

Going Faith (Through Obedience)

Faith is a progression. A growing process.

We see the growth of the Israelites from the banks of the Red Sea to the edge of the Jordan River.

Theirs was a baby step of faith at the Red Sea. They believed, and God parted the waters.

But when they had to cross the Jordan, God required them to show their faith. Once they displayed their faith and dipped their toes into the deep, swirling waters, then the river stopped flowing. They could walk through on dry ground.

The Israelites believed God would equip Moses to part the waters of the sea. But this generation of Israelites entering the Promised Land had to have a greater, trusting faith. They had to show their trust by taking a step of faith, believing God would protect and provide for them, even when everything they could see told a different story.

Faith is an action verb. It is more than just believing; it is acting on the belief we have. I can look at a cute antique chair and believe it will hold me when I sit on it. But that faith is not active until I actually do something with it. I must sit in the chair.

A growing faith is a going faith. It is being obedient to what Jesus asks of us.

One day, Jesus hopped into Simon Peter's boat and asked him to pull out away from the land. Peter had been fishing all night and had nothing to show for it. When Jesus joined him in the boat, Peter was trying to get his nets washed and stored, ready for the next fishing excursion. He was tired; he had worked all night with no fish to show for it. Exhausted by the wearisome labor, Peter only wanted to clean up and head home. But Jesus.

"Simon," Jesus said. "Take the boat out just a little further."

Imagine Peter's tired body dragging back to the boat. Then rowing, rowing, rowing out further so the crowd could hear Jesus teach. Peter must have known how the people needed to hear what Jesus said.

After He finished teaching, Jesus told Peter to put out into the deep and let down the nets for a catch. Peter, exhausted, said, "Master, we toiled all night and took nothing. But at Your word, I will let down the nets" (Luke 5:5 ESV).

Peter obeyed and put the nets down into deeper water. They brought in so many fish the nets began tearing! Amazing things happen when we simply do what Jesus calls us to do. Our faith grows.

We would do well in our faith walk to heed to words of Mary, Jesus' mother:

"Whatever He says to you, do it" (John 2:5).

It sounds so easy, doesn't it? Jesus tells us to go, so we go. He tells us to do this or that, so we do what He says. But it isn't always that simple. We don't always understand why.

I'm always the one in my family to ask "Why?" Curiosity eats at me until I know the reason you want me to go here or there. Why must I do this or that?

But that isn't really faith, is it? Sometimes faith is going without knowing. If that's the case, we can pray like Jehoshaphat: "We do not know what to do, but our eyes are on you" (2 Chronicles 20:12).

We trust in the Lord. Even when we don't know the reason. God is omniscient. He is all-knowing. Nothing is a mystery to Him.

All the more reason to have faith and trust. We bring all our struggles to Him. All our "Whys" and "What ifs." And then we obey. "A whole lot of what we call 'struggling' is simply delayed obedience."[3] So, go when He says "Go!"

Recently, I read through the Bible in 90 days. Whew! Brisk reading of large chunks of scripture can help you see connections you normally wouldn't make.

For instance, when reading through Mark, we see that the word "immediately" appears repeatedly. In many of the passages, it describes people who are doing what Jesus asked of them. They didn't do it later, or tomorrow. They didn't wait until next week, or when it was convenient. Immediately, they obeyed.

Our obedience needs to be immediate. Don't hesitate.

Faith Becomes Sight

In my journeys, Mesa Verde taught me to look up. When we traveled to Moab, Utah, I learned another important lesson.

In Moab, the landscapes were breathtaking. Everywhere we looked, there were soaring rock pinnacles, massive fins of stone, and giant boulders, balancing on nothing (or so it seemed!). It was a red-rock wonderland. Our favorite spots were Canyonlands and Arches National Parks.

Though we are not fitness buffs, we opted to hike the hard, rocky terrain. It was a rough uphill climb. I focused on every rock that could trip me up. Instead, I should have focused on seeing the beautiful rock formations in front of me.

Reaching the plateau, I looked out and saw a grand vista of mesas painted with violet, blue, and terracotta from God's color palate. I almost missed it because my focus was on the "what if" rocks. What if I stumble over these big rocks because I wasn't looking down?

Looking around, I saw the towering rock structures. They brought to mind Psalm 61:2, which says, "Lead me to the rock that is higher than I." It made me think of how God is like a towering rock, always above and protecting me. He can see things from His vantage point that I cannot, and never will.

Finally, my mustard seed faith had become sight. Instead of looking down and worrying about the large boulders that may trip me, I knew what I needed to do: look out and see the possibilities of unfaltering, rock-solid faith in Jesus.

When faith becomes sight, it takes root and thrives in us.

When our faith becomes sight, it takes root and thrives in us. As we step out in obedience to Him, we trust Jesus is watching over us. We trust God's eternal plan will make all things right.

Golden Faith (Yielded)

Just as a growing faith leads to a going (obedient) faith, a going faith leads to a golden faith. As in golden maturity. Faith leads to obedience, and obedience leads to maturity and yielding to God.

Jesus is a beautiful example of this in the Garden of Gethsemane (Matthew 26:39-46), where He was praying before He went to the cross.

Jesus falls face down in reverence to God to pray. The suffering Jesus was about to endure grieved Him.

His first request to God was, in essence, *If it's possible, don't make me walk through this. Take this hard thing away.* However, Jesus ends this prayer with *Not My will, but Yours.*

He's saying what I've said in many a prayer, "Please don't make me do it!" Sadly, I don't always include, "Not my will but Yours, sweet Lord..."

The second time Jesus prays, He says, *If You can't take it away, if I must walk through it, let Your will be done.* He knows anything is possible with God, that His Father CAN take it away, but also that God's will must be done. And if it's God's will that this should happen, then Jesus must walk it. There's a slight shift from "let it pass from Me" to "if it can't", almost as if He is saying, "So be it."

The genuine change of heart comes the third time Jesus prays. We see that God's will became Jesus's will. Jesus had reconciled His heart to the will of His Father. Not only that, we see in Matthew 26:45-46 (CSB) Jesus embraces God's will for Him: "The time is near...Get up! Let's go!" Jesus submits completely to God's will and is ready to go to the cross.

Faith that is growing, obedient, and yielded to God is a scary thing. The good news is, we don't have to travel this path alone. We have the grace of Jesus available to us. And His grace is sufficient (2 Corinthians 2:9).

It's often said that God in His grace gives us what we do not deserve (the free gift of salvation) and in His mercy, He does not give us what we actually deserve (death and separation from Him). What is this "grace" that is sufficient? It is God's provision for our every need when we need it. Warren Wiersbe says, "if God's grace is sufficient to save us, surely it is sufficient to keep us and strengthen us in our times of suffering."[4]

Grace is God's supernatural provision for our every need when we need it. It is the spiritual empowerment God gives to believers. This spiritual enabling (grace) is a gift that we too often reach for as a last resort. Growing in the grace and knowledge of Jesus (2 Peter 3:18) will help us reach out to Him first.

When we walk in faith, we are not alone. In our weakness, God meets us with an abundance of grace. And it is sufficient.

Walking in Faith

The writer of Hebrews tells us faith is the surety of what we hope for and the evidence of things we can't see. We cannot please God—it's impossible—without faith (Hebrews 11:1, 6).

Several years ago, John and I planned a photography vacation in Arizona so he could take some breathtaking pictures of the scenery.

Horseshoe Bend was the one photo John really, really wanted to capture. It was a three-quarter-mile hike over a hot, arid trail of sand. Temperatures hovered above 100 degrees. The overlook was 4,200 feet above sea level, which made it a tough hike for these two South Louisiana tourists!

The observation point had a guardrail so you could safely see the breathtaking view of the Colorado River 1,000 feet below. There was also an area of the cliff with no guardrails and huge rocks to climb up to get an even better view of the river. It was a sheer drop straight down! Having a fear of heights, I stayed away from this area, but John wanted to climb on the rocks, hang over the edge, and get the best picture of Horseshoe Bend. I begged him not to do it.

Near us was a young Asian couple on the cliff top with obviously the same problem. With camera in hand, he wanted to walk to the edge of the cliff. She was in distress!

In a shrill voice, full of fear, I could almost see the Japanese hieroglyphics shooting out of her mouth. The words blasted her husband, and he took note of her fear.

I looked John dead in the eye, pointed to the young woman and said, "YEAH, what SHE said!"

Loosely translated, I'm pretty sure she was saying, "DON'T DO IT! Please don't go to the edge! You could fall! I would be a widow! I hope you have your insurance paid up!"

John didn't listen to me. He walked around the bend, out of my sight, up the rocks, stood on the edge of the cliff (with no guardrails!), and took the most stunning picture of Horseshoe Bend.

Sometimes you have to stand at the edge of the cliff (or with your toes in the flood waters) to see the vast landscape and experience how God will provide. Sometimes your baby steps of faith need to grow into giant leaps, trusting Jesus. This pleases Him.

Immediately after Mama had the stroke, I prayed without ceasing, "Lord, heal my Mama." And He answered that prayer. Mama rebounded and was better. But then she would crash again. It was a vicious cycle.

To be honest, I was praying selfishly. I was fearful and didn't want Mama to die. I wasn't ready for her to leave us. Looking at Mama's health, I only saw through my limited perspective. I didn't have faith in God's timing, nor trust He knew what was best for her. I was on the edge of the cliff.

While I was "what if-ing" my Mama's stroke, hospice care, and how long she would be with us, God knew exactly the number of her days. He had my Mama in His strong, capable hands.

Soon, I had a perspective change. I considered Mama's health and stroke from an eternal point of view. At that point, I could pray like Jesus.

"Lord not my will, but Yours."

And as my faith and trust grew, I could pray like this:

"Lord, heal Mama completely. No matter what that looks like on earth. No matter if that means bringing her home to You. Heal her completely."

And He did. Jesus answered my prayer of faith that was yielded to Him. He also gave me a glimpse of my Mama's faith. It was what I would call grandiose. Her faith was colossal and impressive. Why? Because she knew—no matter what!—that Jesus would bring her home to Him.

Exiles rejoice when their faith is growing, going, golden, and grandiose!

• • • ● ● • ● • • •

Stepping Stone #10

REJOICE:
You are an exile with active and growing faith.

REFLECT on God's Word:
1 Corinthians 2:13
2 Corinthians 2:9

RESPOND to the questions:

- Was there a time in your life that your faith had a growth spurt? What prompted the growth? Reflect on that time, praising God for His faithfulness!

- Did you know God's grace is His supernatural enabling within us? Describe a time you experienced this supernatural enabling. What did God empower you to do in His strength?

- Have your prayers ever had a perspective change by moving from praying your will to praying for God's will? If not, how can you make this change in your prayer life?

Chapter 11

REJOICING IN CONFIDENCE

*We don't seek to escape this life by dreaming of heaven. But we do
find we can endure this life because of the certainty of heaven.*
~John MacArthur

I T WAS CERTAIN DEATH. Shadrach, Meshach, and Abed-nego
were to be thrown into fiery flames. The king had ordered the
furnace to be heated seven times more than normal (Daniel 3:19).
No man could survive that! But there was no other option.

King Nebuchadnezzar built a massive golden idol that soared
ninety feet into the air. Its size impressed many of the people. But
what was its purpose? They didn't have to wait long to find out.

The king's heralds announced, "When you hear the music playing, you are to fall down and worship this idol of the king" (Daniel
3:5, my paraphrase). Not a problem for most people. But Shadrach,
Meshach, and Abed-nego were not most people. They were Jews
living in servitude to the people of Babylon. They were in exile. God
had sent them there. It was Him—the one true God—they served,
even in exile.

Thinking back, they knew exactly when Nebuchadnezzar became
so angered.

"Will the three of you fall down and worship this idol? If not, you are going to be thrown into the furnace of fire! And what god can rescue you from my hands and the penalty I impose?" said the king (Daniel 3:14-15, my paraphrase).

The three replied, "Our God is able. He's going to bring us out of the fire. And you know what? Even if He doesn't, we won't worship your image or your gods" (Daniel 3:17-18, my paraphrase).

Yep, that's exactly what set old Nebbie off (remember, I like nicknames). His face puffed up, turning bright red. Bulging, his eyes looked like they were ready to pop out of the sockets. And there was smoke coming out of his ears. Or maybe that was the furnace?

"Throw them in the fire!" the king bellowed. The flames were so hot, they killed the men who carried the three to certain death. Ruh-roh! Surely it would kill Shadrach, Meshach, and Abed-nego, too. Wouldn't it?

It was a living hell, literally. Do you remember from Chapter 7 how scripture describes hell? As a furnace of fire (Matthew 13:42, 50). Only there was one key difference for Shadrach, Meshach, and Abed-nego. God was with them.

Confidence in Rescue

Confidence poured out of Shadrach, Meshach, and Abed-nego. They had an "even if" mindset versus a "what if" mindset. How? Because of the great faith they placed in God.

These three would never bow down and worship a mute, lifeless idol. Why should they? Their God is alive! God sees them and knows them. He walks with them, even through fiery flames. They believed God could reach in and snatch them from the furnace.

Their confidence came from knowing God was always with them. They had no reason to fear or tremble. Shadrach, Meshach, and Abed-nego didn't believe for a minute that they could save themselves. Their hope was not in friends who, at the last minute, would sweep in and rescue them.

What happened in the furnace? God happened. He protected them in the fire. Even the king saw it (Daniel 3:25). "Didn't I only throw three men in the fire? I see four men walking around!"

Shadrach, Meshach, and Abed-nego knew God could rescue them from a fiery death. But even if He didn't, they would still keep their eyes on Him and worship Him alone.

Why?

After all, God had exiled them to Babylon. Weren't they mad? Didn't they hold a grudge? Apparently not.

They placed their confidence in God and His power to save them. In the struggles, suffering, and trials of life, they knew God would be with them.

God never promises we will have a life free from trials and troubles. Matter of fact, scripture says unequivocally that God's people will suffer. Peter tells us we are called to suffer. Paul wrote in no uncertain terms of his suffering. Scripture celebrates the suffering of martyrs. Even our Savior, Jesus, suffered. Hmmm, that's a calling I don't particularly want, amen? But God's Word is truth, and we must be prepared to go through a fiery furnace. Persecution will come and we will suffer for Jesus' sake and for the gospel.[1]

Who will we turn to when the trials come? Can any human deliver us? Can we have faith in their abilities? Or our own? Oh, it may seem that men are helping us. But God. He is the One who is able. He directs men to go and do His will. Our confidence is in Him.

He is the only one who can rescue us.

Look back at your life. Have you suffered? Can you see how God delivered you from the trial?

Are you suffering now? Will you watch expectantly to see what the Lord will do?

Are you prepared to suffer in the future? Are you confident the Lord will bring you through?

God has delivered us in the past. He is delivering us now, in the present, and He will deliver us from the storms we can't yet see (2 Corinthians 1:10).

When we look back and remember God's faithfulness, we can watch with great anticipation to see what He will do now, and we can rest confidently in the assurance that He will indeed deliver us in the future.

When suffering comes (and it will), we can say like the prophet Micah, "I will watch expectantly for the LORD; I will wait for the God of my salvation. My God will hear me" (Micah 7:7).

That's what Daniel's friends were doing in the fire. Watching and waiting expectantly on God, knowing He is able.

We can have that confident assurance, too.

Rescued and Relocated

Assurance is being certain in our minds and having freedom from doubts or uncertainty. It is being secure in our confidence in God. Because not only is He in control, He sent Jesus, our hope.

Peter, in his letter to the exiled church (in other words, us!), calls this hope "living."

Hope, by itself, is expecting something. It's the desire of some good, with the expectation of receiving it. When we place our hope in Jesus, we expect that something good will come of it. That "something good" is our salvation.

Jesus rescued us from the power of sin. It holds no authority in our lives because of Jesus. He is more powerful than any sin that tempts us, and He is our ultimate authority. That's good news! Jesus also saved us from the penalty of sin, which is death. Our living hope is trust and confidence in Jesus because He lives! And one day we will live with Him.

Paul tells the church at Corinth, "If we have hoped in Christ in this life only, we are of all men most to be pitied" (1 Corinthians 15:19). We must have a confident hope in the life to come.

Jesus rose from the dead to give us confidence that we will have eternal life in Him. He is called the firstfruits of those who have died. This is a reference to Leviticus 23:9-14, where the priests would wave the first bundles of the wheat harvest before the Lord. This was a sign the entire harvest belonged to God. Therefore, if Christ is the first of the harvest of men, and He is resurrected, He will be the first of many. Jesus will harvest (resurrect) all those who believe in Him and belong to Him. I like the way the New Living Translation states it. Jesus "is the first of a great harvest of all who have died" (1 Corinthians 15:20 NLT).

> *Our confident hope is living. It grows larger and more beautiful as time goes on.*

Why does Peter call this hope living? Something that is living has life. *Yes, that's pretty obvious, Ellen. So what?* Something that has life grows. Our confident hope is living. It grows larger and more beautiful as time goes on. It becomes more glorious.

Last year I planted some Old Fashioned Cockscomb seeds. It took several weeks, but they finally sprouted. They grew an inch or so, then stalled. There was no growth. I transferred them to a larger pot, so the roots had room to expand. Still, nothing. And then the rains came. The more those seeds got watered by God, the more they grew. They were living, and they were glorious! The deeper our faith in Jesus, the more confidence we have in Him and His plans for us. Our confidence grows as our love and trust for Him grows.

As exiles here, we walk in confidence that Jesus has rescued us from death and Satan's power over us. It's an eternal do-over!

Jesus also rescues us by relocating us. He moves us from darkness to light. The darkness here is spiritual darkness, the evil of this world. The Bible describes it as rulers, powers, and "spiritual forces of wickedness in the heavenly places" (Ephesians 6:12). That's enough to make me want to move. How about you? The spiritual darkness is pervading our world, our country, and our neighborhoods. To dispel the darkness, we need more light. As followers of Jesus, we shine brightly for Him.

Where does Christ move us? Into the kingdom of God (Colossians 1:13), or the kingdom of Heaven. We weren't just moved from darkness to light. God calls us out of the darkness! He beckons us to come from the darkness that surrounds us into His marvelous light (1 Peter 2:9). The word marvelous in the original Greek means to marvel.[2] The light of Christ is so wondrous we can't help but be in awe of it and marvel at it. His light draws us. When we have Jesus' light in us, it attracts people to Him.

My husband and I have an acquaintance who is a professed atheist. This person knows the gospel truth but chooses not to surrender to the call of God. We don't try to convert him or preach to him. We love him and pray for him. The amazing thing? He doesn't avoid us because of our love for Jesus. Matter of fact, he keeps coming to visit. Over and over. Like a moth to a porch light. We remain confident that God will work in his life as He did in the life of the King of Babylon.

Confidence in Adversity

Raise your hand if you've ever been through any kind of tragedy, trial, or adversity. Yep, I saw a lot of hands raised, mine included.

We can withstand adversity. We can even be confident in adversity when we understand the truth of who God is. Our God is sovereign. This means God is in control over all creatures, all occurrences, and all circumstances. Not only that, He is in control of all things all the time (Isaiah 14:24, 46:10). When trouble comes, God knows about it. We need not fear the future. He is in command of the universe as well as our lives.

The Lord was so faithful to show me His sovereignty when my mom had her stroke. When I got the call that she was in the hospital, John and I immediately headed to Mississippi. It sounds easy. Take I-10 east to I-55, then go north. Oh, but the traffic in Baton Rouge!

It is a conundrum. Going west on any day was not bad. Driving east was a different story. Several bottlenecks jammed up traffic. We got stuck in one of those tangled gridlocks years before. We moved slower and slower until at last we came to a dead stop. Our GPS flashed a message:

"Would you like to switch to pedestrian mode?"

Well, no, we certainly would not!

That day, on our way to see Mama, we could see traffic was backing up near Baton Rouge.

"What do you want to do?" John asked.

"I don't know. I just know we can't get stuck for one to two hours in traffic. What are our options?"

"I can see if the GPS will recommend another route."

The alternate route took us through small towns that dotted the map north of Baton Rouge and kept us out of the bottlenecks. It was the most peaceful drive! We meandered along, without the stress of heavy stop-and-go traffic, and ended up...on I-55 north! We lost no time on our new route!

I sensed God whispering to me:

Sweet Ellen, I had your back the whole time. If you had gone through Baton Rouge, I would have cleared the way. But I also provided you an alternate route, so that you would not have driving stresses. Either way, I was with you. Haven't I told you in My Word? I will make darkness into light before them, and rugged places into plains (cf Isaiah 42:16).

The Lord provided what I needed when I needed it. He was in control throughout that trial.

God, in His sovereignty, allows trials. He doesn't cause our troubles, and He is certainly powerful enough to keep them from happening. But because the outcomes belong to Him, we can look for His purpose. God has a purpose for every adversity we face.

> ### *Hardships and suffering grow our faith.*

God allows us to face trials so we will seek Him. Adversity can either turn us inward toward despair or force us to focus on God. When we focus on Him through afflictions, we become dependent on Him. We know God is aware of our situation and will work all things for good. In this way, hardships and suffering can grow our trust in God. The more confidence we have in Him, the more our faith grows.

With Jesus walking beside us, we can be confident in adversity. We are confident that Jesus holds us in His hands and will never let us go.

Glenna Marshall explains: "God has used my physical suffering and mental anguish to pull my heart toward eternity."[3]

Over and over, we see that God never wastes our pain. He uses it to pull us toward Him and eternity. He uses it to strengthen our confidence in Him.

Our pain, when suffered with joy, brings glory to God, our Father. When our faith is tested, it grows our endurance (James 1:3). Trials, troubles, and tribulations strengthen us to persevere, grow our character, and give us hope for our life to come (Romans 5:3-4).

Result of Confident Assurance

When we walk in confident assurance in Jesus and what He has done for us, we will reap many benefits, the first of which is no lack. Nothing will be missing in our lives. No insufficiencies, because Jesus is all-sufficient. He will provide all that we need. Remember what He told His disciples in Luke 22?

"'When I sent you out without money belt and bag and sandals, you did not lack anything, did you?' They said, 'No, nothing'" (Luke 22:35). He still provides for us today.

Paul tells us that in everything, we are "enriched in Him, in all speech and all knowledge," so that we will not lack in any gift (1 Corinthians 1:5,7).

And James, the brother of Jesus, tells us to "count it all joy" (James 1:2-4) when we suffer, go through trials, or feel like we are in a fiery furnace. He tells us these trials will produce endurance, or perseverance. And "if perseverance goes full-term it will develop a thoroughly mature Christian who lacks nothing. He will indeed be all God wants him to be."[4]

> *We will not be shaken when we walk with Jesus and allow Him to guide us.*

We will not be shaken when we walk with Jesus and allow Him to guide us (Psalm 16:8). Our confidence is that His presence is with us, and His power is available to us. Nothing can rattle us.

With Jesus, we can face any battle with confidence.

Have you ever been in a battle? I've had some skirmishes in my lifetime. Some I won, others not so much. One battle was with a sweet lady in our church. Who knew little old church ladies could be so fierce? But that feisty lady taught me a thing or two about battle.

First, I did not prepare for conflict. I assumed things would just blow over. Second, I underestimated my opponent.

It is a spiritual battle we face each day. We must prepare for it. We prepare when we stand firm in our faith by standing firm in the Lord (1 Corinthians 16:13, Philippians 4:1). This means trusting in Him and placing our confidence in Him, not ourselves. The Lord has given us weapons (Ephesians 6:11-14) to use in battle. We stand firm when we dress in God's armor each day. Psalm 18 tells us God has clothed us with strength for the battle (Psalm 18:32, 29).

Don't underestimate your enemy. My enemy was not this sweet, yet fierce, church lady. My battle was not against any earthly being. Today, we fight a supernatural war, and our enemy is Satan. He doesn't stand for truth. He is a liar and the father of lies. Know your opponent, make a battle plan, put on your armor, and then fight with confidence! Jesus won the war when He defeated death on the cross. Remember, then, that we are not fighting for victory, but <u>from</u> victory!

When we walk closely with Jesus, we won't lack confidence, ability, or provision. We will stand firm and nothing will shake us. But we don't walk with Jesus and stand firm in Him to claim glory for ourselves. What resulted from the confidence Shadrach, Meshach, and Abed-nego had in God? God got the glory!

King Nebuchadnezzar saw a fourth man in the fire with Daniel's friends. He knew their God was in the fire with them, protecting them. So Nebuchadnezzar praised God saying, "Blessed be the God of Shadrach, Meshach and Abed-nego, who has sent His angel and delivered His servants who put their trust in Him,...there is no other god who is able to deliver in this way" (Daniel 3:28-29).

Our strong confidence in God's ability to rescue and relocate us gives us strength to withstand adversity. This brings glory to God. How? We honor God with our victories and praise Him for winning the battle. We tell others what He has done for us and what He will do for them.

Losing and Gaining Confidence

What happens then, if we lose our confidence?

> *When confidence slips, Satan slithers in.*

When confidence slips, Satan slithers in.

After her death, I realized I had lost so much more than Mama. Little bits of me and my childhood were gone. Thinking back, I couldn't remember details of my younger life. Little things that only a mother would remember. Losing that was like losing myself.

Then one day, a Bible teacher was talking about our salvation experience.

"It's a point in time in your life. Your salvation is a specific event in your life, the moment you said yes to Jesus. It is something you will remember and can say with confidence: 'This is the day of my salvation.'"

A cold dread filled my heart. I could not remember the specifics of when I said yes to Jesus. Oh, I remember my baptism. I stepped down into the baptistry, a child of eleven. Or was it twelve? I remember the little sleeveless shift dress I wore. It had tiny yellow flowers scattered over it. My Mama made that dress, and to make it "fancy" she added small yellow bows to each side near the hem.

I remember when Mama and Daddy sat down with me and my brother, asking if we were ready. I knew what they meant. They were talking about walking the aisle and making my faith in Jesus public.

But I could not remember exactly when I said "Yes" to Jesus.

"Yes, I trust You to save me. Yes, I believe You died on the cross for me. Yes, I believe I will have eternal life. Yes, I'm a sinner and I need You, Jesus!"

For the life of me, I had no clue. There was only one person I could ask. And she was gone.

Mama remembered everything.

My confidence in my salvation waned. When was I saved? Was it as a child, before I was baptized? Or was it after my baptism, as an adult, when I returned to the Lord after years of wilderness wandering? Am I saved now?

As my confidence slipped, Satan slid in, maintaining a steady assault on my assurance of salvation. He saw an opening to cause chaos and gleefully grabbed hold of it.

Like the serpent in Eden, I heard him whisper, "Are you really saved?"

It was a spiritual battle I did not expect. Satan cast doubts that made me question the certainty of my eternal life. My doubts marred my hope of Heaven. If Heaven was a giant whiteboard, my doubts would have been a huge X that crossed its surface.

It wasn't a constant battle. The doubts would come and go.

"Lord," I pleaded, "Help me remember. Give me a confirmation, any kind of confirmation, of what point in time You saved me! Please, Lord!"

I stormed Heaven. Because of my faith in Jesus, I went boldly into God's presence, asking for His help, knowing He is able.

Prayer, God's Word, and the counsel of godly friends. That's what it took to find my confidence.

By studying God's Word and listening to my pastor preach truth, I realized I was saved as a child. For a time, I wandered in the wilderness and weeds grew up. But God is my Gardener, and He yanked those weeds right out of my heart!

God is the Gardener of our souls and will pull every weed from our hearts.

However, I still had no memory of saying "Yes" to Jesus. I am confident of my salvation, but just can't remember the details. After all, it had been decades. In her book, *Grace Maps: Our Journey Guided by God's Grace,* my friend Carmen Horne suggested I write about how I remembered Jesus as a child. [5]

"What was He like to you?" she asked.

"I don't know! We went to church, I remember that, but I don't have memories of Jesus."

Oh, but God. He is able.

Amid my doubts, our church had a revival. On the last night of our church's revival, over fifty people decided to be baptized and took the plunge during the "baptism night." Dozens walked the aisle and publicly gave their life to Jesus. They went to the baptistry right then and there to be fully immersed in the waters, an outward sign of their inward faith in Jesus.

Suddenly, I noticed the sweet family in front of us. I watched as the oldest daughter crumpled in tears, surrendered to Jesus, and walked forward to profess her faith in Christ. Then, the younger sister began to weep as she submitted her life as well.

I was crying with them. It was a beautiful sight to see. But it also brought back a memory for me. We always watched the Billy Graham crusades when I was a child. One night, during the invitation and singing the hymn "Just As I Am" I remember weeping on the couch, my heart yielded in surrender to Jesus. The Lord God drew me to Him that night. I have every confidence that He saved me that night!

God is able. He was with me through this fire of doubt. He helped me overcome Satan's lies. And He brought back a memory that was over fifty years old!

If your confidence wanes, keep praying! Stay connected with believers. And know that even if you can't see Jesus' hand in your life, you know His heart.

Overcomers

Shadrach, Meshach, and Abed-nego were overcomers as well. They made it through the fiery furnace unharmed because God was by their side. They had confidence in His abilities.

And with Jesus, we are overcomers. We are victorious over Satan by the blood of the Lamb and the word of our testimony (Revelation 12:11). We will trust Jesus and tell of His faithfulness even until death. We have already overcome the evil one (1 John 2:13, 1 John 4:4) and the world (1 John 5:4-5) with our faith, trust, and confident assurance in Jesus.

In Hebrews, the writer tells us to hold on to our confidence, as it will be richly rewarded (Hebrews 10:35). Jesus tells us about these blessings in Revelation. He assures us that overcomers will not be hurt by the second death (Revelation 2:11, i.e. the Lake of Fire, or hell). Jesus tells us that as victors, the Book of Life will always have our names in it. They will never be erased.

But the best thing? We will sit next to Jesus: "He who overcomes, I will grant to him to sit down with Me on My throne, as I also overcame and sat down with My Father on His throne" (Revelation 3:21). With Jesus as our Living Hope, we are overcomers and conquerors. When we have doubts, we can come to Him with assurance and confidence. Not in ourselves, not because we're perfect, but because He is. He will provide and guide us into all truth.

In Christ, we can move from an attitude of "what if" to "even if" and walk in "holy confidence and humble obedience."[6] As exiles, we can walk with our heads held high as we journey toward home.

• • • ● ● ● ● • • •

Stepping Stone #11

REJOICE:

You are an exile whose confidence is in God, not man.

REFLECT on God's Word:

Daniel 3

1 Peter 2:9

RESPOND to the questions:

- Where do you place your confidence: in your abilities, the ability of others, or in God? Why?

- What fiery furnaces have you walked through in your life? Did the trial bring you closer to Jesus? In what ways did you feel His presence with you?

- Has your confidence in Jesus ever wavered? What happened? What caused you to regain your confidence?

Chapter 12

REJOICING WHILE YOU LONG FOR HOME

Maybe at the heart of all our traveling is the dream of someday,
somehow, getting Home.
~Frederick Buechner

THE BEGINNING OF THE end. I've written the beginning of
this final chapter a dozen times and changed it a dozen times.
It's a struggle.

We realize we are strangers who don't belong here and recognize
Heaven is our home. But really, how do we rejoice as exiles?

Honestly, I'm still struggling to have a heavenly mindset. I cling to
this world too much. I'm attached to it. When Mama had her stroke,
and I was traveling back and forth from Louisiana to Mississippi and
back again, I had one foot in both worlds. I struggle with that now,
torn between my loyalty to Heaven and my attachment to earth.

Aren't we all? There is a conflict in our hearts: living lives that are
homebound versus homeward.

We <u>are</u> heavenly-minded. But we also love this life the Lord has
given us. Even with all its trials and tribulations, it is hard to imagine
better than this. Many times, our hearts lean toward home. Longing

to see our loved ones again will tug our hearts toward home. The empty ache we feel inside draws us toward home. Yet we firmly plant ourselves here. What keeps pulling us back to earth?

I think it's the unknown. Sitting on the patio yesterday, I watched it rain. What will that be like on the new earth? Will it even rain? Will the weather always be perfect? What about the mosquitoes? Will they bite? So much we don't know and can't imagine, even though we know Heaven is home and we are exiles here.

How can we live as exiles who long for home?

Elizabeth Elliot's advice will serve us well: Just do the next thing. "Whatever that is, just do the next thing. God will meet you there."[1] Eventually, your heart will follow your mind.

Practical Living as an Exile

Doing the next thing often involves simply being practical.

Practically speaking, what's the best way to live as an exile?

Like Joseph and Daniel, bloom where God plants you! God will bring beauty from the ashes of our circumstances.

The prophet Jeremiah gives excellent guidance to those living as exiles longing to go home. He spoke the exact opposite of other prophets, who were falsely predicting a short exile. Those guys were misleading the Jewish people into thinking they would be home sooner rather than later. They incorrectly proclaimed the exile would be short.

Don't worry, you'll be home in no time! Sit tight. It was a message that made the people feel good.

However, Jeremiah spoke God's truth, which on the surface wasn't quite as comforting.

You won't return home until after the seventy years God has ordained is complete. Then Jeremiah offers some practical advice straight from God Himself:

"Build houses and live in them; and plant gardens and eat their produce. Take wives and become the fathers of sons and daughters, and take wives for your sons and give your daughters to husbands, that they may bear sons and daughters; and multiply there and do not decrease. Seek the welfare of the city where I have sent you into exile, and pray to the LORD on its behalf; for in its welfare you will have welfare" (Jeremiah 29:5-7).

Jeremiah's word from God was telling them to settle down and make a life for themselves. But doesn't settling down defeat the purpose of living eternally-minded lives? Wouldn't settling down mean digging our roots deeper into this world?

Not if we follow Daniel's example. Daily, he prayed, looking toward home through his open window. For Daniel, facing Jerusalem to pray was a physical reminder that he wasn't home. Prayer drew him toward home spiritually. Daniel hoped to return home one day, both in a physical and a spiritual sense. Each day, we can orient ourselves toward home through prayer.

We won't become deeply rooted in the world if we remember a couple of things. First, we own nothing on this earth. Second, everything we have comes from God. Every good and perfect gift is from above (James 1:17). We are simply stewards of God's property until He brings us to our forever home.

We blossom and grow where God plants us, and spread seeds of faith and hope to those around us.

The Israelites in Babylon knew they would be home again one day. God had promised them. We have that same promise. Doesn't it make sense, then, to settle down for the temporary stay? Live here, where God has placed us. Have a successful life and beautiful house, but know that our actual home is waiting. Blossom and grow where God plants us, and spread seeds of faith and hope to those around us. His plan is to prosper us and not to harm us. He gives us a hope and a future. When God settles us into a strange land (no matter how temporary), it could be His place of promise for us.

Jeremiah goes one step further and offers spiritual advice. He tells the exiles to pray for the city where God placed them. Pray on its behalf and seek its welfare (Jeremiah 29:7).

I will not sugarcoat things now. Praying for the place and the people holding us captive can be very hard. Just look around. Is crime running rampant? Do we always agree with the leadership? Does it seem as if evil is all around us? After watching the evening news, would you rather pack it all up and move off the grid? I would! But I have accepted that the Lord placed me here, in this place, at this time, for His purposes. So I have chosen some scriptures to pray especially for our culture.

"Break the arm of the wicked and the evildoer, seek out his wickedness until You find none" (Psalm 10:15).

Now, I don't think the Lord wants us running around breaking people's arms. Although seeing the wickedness all around us, I would be okay with a little physical tussle every now and then. When God breaks the arm of the sinister person, I believe He is limiting the far-reaching effects of their evil. A broken arm can't reach very far, can it?

The Psalms give us more prayer weapons. They tell us to "let the evil of the wicked come to an end" (Psalm 7:9) and "You have destroyed the wicked" (Psalm 9:5). Is God going to wipe out all the evil and wicked people by killing them? In the words of the apostle Paul, "May it never be!" What, then, is God's heart?

"'As I live!' declares the Lord GOD, 'I take no pleasure in the death of the wicked, but rather that the wicked turn from his way and live'" (Ezekiel 33:11).

> *Settle down where God places you, but don't get too comfortable.*

The Lord's heart is that all should come to know Jesus and live. That is why we pray for the place that has us in exile. We pray purposeful kingdom prayers. Our prayer is that the wicked person will turn away from evil, come to know and love Jesus, and long for the better home He has for them. If we want to save our country, we pray for our countrymen to be saved.

So, for the time being, we settle down. But we don't get too comfy and cozy.

Don't Get Comfortable

We don't get comfortable because it's all temporary. The weekend we purged Mama's house brought this reality home to me.

It was poignant. Going through her things. Some of it we recognized and memories flooded us. The large baking sheet my daddy always used at Thanksgiving when he made his homemade yeast rolls. The old cast iron piggy bank that was always in the kitchen, covered with a film of grease and grit. Mama's needlepoint hanging on the wall, proclaiming, "This is the day the Lord has made!"

Other things were a mystery. Maybe gifts from friends? Or from an old aunt who had downsized? The most heart wrenching of all, though, was the pile of trash. Years of accumulated "stuff." To be thrown out. Into the garbage. Gone. Like Mama.

There has to be more! My heart ached. I knew Mama was more than piles of trash. I knew she was more than stuff. She was a living human being who had touched people's lives. And yet, these garbage bags and a few mementos were all that remained. I could touch these things, but they weren't Mama. They weren't her hands I could hold, or her voice I could hear each week saying, "Hey darlin'!" Only memories remained.

Wonderful memories. But memories that will fade away in time. Temporary. King David recognized this. In 1 Chronicles 29:15, he said, "We are sojourners...our days on earth are like a passing shadow, gone so soon without a trace."

In order for our days here on earth to count, we must not become too comfortable. Comfort leads to complacency. Indifferent, apathetic, and lukewarm. Sleeping on the job. Too comfortable to care. Content with where we are. That's complacency. It is unimaginable to me how someone could be apathetic towards God and all the incredible things He has done for us.

Apathy consumes us, causing us to live short-sighted lives. We see only the immediate. But God has better things for us. He has a place prepared for us when the time is right. How can our hearts grow cold to this? With hard hearts, we are in danger of spiritual sluggishness, like the church in Thessalonica.

Paul wrote to the church at Thessalonica to encourage the new believers. They were suffering persecution and wrongly assumed

God's judgment had begun. The result of this incorrect teaching was that many of the believers stopped working and decided to just sit and wait for Christ's return.[2]

It reminds me of the story my mom told of her Daddy's old mule. He would use the mule to help plow up the fields for planting. So many times that old mule would just STOP in the middle of a row. No more plowing. He wouldn't budge an inch. I suppose he was tired and decided to just wait out in the field for someone to unhitch him and take him home to the barn.

I imagine the Christians at Thessalonica felt this way. They assumed that since Jesus' return was imminent, it was logical not to work anymore. So they stopped. Stubborn as a mule, you might say.

Haven't we all been at this point occasionally? So discouraged and tired we just want to quit? Too comfortable to move forward and too complacent to do anything about it. Sluggish like a slimy snail.

> *Exiles guard against spiritual sluggishness.*

Paul urges them (1 Thessalonians 5:6) not to sleep as others do. He's talking about being spiritually asleep, unconcerned about sin, and careless in performing their duties and work. As exiles, we must guard against spiritual sluggishness.

Filling our minds with "the noise of the world" will put us to sleep spiritually.[3] Paul tells us to awaken and be alert (1 Thessalonians 5:6, Romans 13:11). Don't get lulled back into the world. Don't sleepwalk through life. Know that you are headed home, and examine yourself. Do you want to take the shortcut, idly waiting for Jesus? Or do you want to take the scenic route, experiencing the awe and beauty of the Lord along the journey?

As young kids, traveling with our parents, they urged us to sleep most of the trip. Easier on them, I'm sure! But when we were almost there, they would wake us up.

"Look at the beach! See the waves? Look! A dolphin! Wake up! You're missing it!"

We are almost home. Don't sleep through the best part of life. God is still working in our world. Open your eyes to see His wonder all around you.

> ***When we long for home, we emulate Jesus.***

Was the church at Thessalonica wrong to long for home and the return of Christ? Is it okay for us to long for Heaven? Won't that make us dissatisfied and discontent with where we are?

No, because when we long for home, we emulate Jesus.

Almost Home

He was almost home. Oh, how He missed sitting next to His Father. Jesus yearned to be there.

He knew a little something about being a stranger. After all, He was fully human and fully God. As God, He didn't quite fit in with this world. Matter of fact, He was born to die. That was His purpose in life—to come to earth and die for the sins of the world. Who else can say this? But Jesus knew there was a better place for Him. A place where He belonged and would return to when His mission on earth was complete.

In this place, His Father knew and still knows Him. Son of God, King of Kings, Lord of Lords. The Messiah, Redeemer of the world. All the identities He left behind, the more glorious identities.

Like the returning exiles, Jesus knew there was a better future ahead. For Him and all the saints the Father has given Him, there is eternal life! A new Heaven and earth. Paradise. Blissful perfection.

Home. Soon He would return to His one true home. A better home than any here on earth. How did He know this? Because He had been there, seated at the right hand of God. Before Bethlehem, Jesus was one with God the Father. They worked together. But Jesus set His glory aside to become one with us.

"And now, Father, glorify Me in Your own presence with the glory that I had with You before the world existed" (John 17:15 ESV).

Jesus' great desire was to return to the prior glory He knew seated next to God. It wasn't to elevate Himself for honor or praise. He longed for home because that's where He belonged—with His Father.

But, Jesus had work to finish on earth. His death on the cross completed His mission from the Father (John 17:4). Jesus asked God for the glory He knew before so He "might glorify the Father in His return to Heaven."[4]

When it was His time, Jesus set His face like flint, looking neither to the right nor to the left. He focused on His purpose. It gave Him joy. "For the joy set before Him (He) endured the cross, despising the shame, and has sat down at the right hand of the throne of God" (Hebrews 12:2). The joy of Heaven far outweighed the pain of the cross.

And what was this joy that awaited Jesus?

Bringing glory to God the Father. Being able to sit once again at the right hand of God's throne. Jesus knows that any pain and suffering He faces is nothing compared to being right next to His Father.

With great joy, Jesus longed for home.

What about us? How do we live while we wait?

While We Wait

It's hard to imagine that the apostle Peter could give us practical advice. After all, he was headstrong and impulsive, quite impetuous. Whether right or wrong, Peter always spoke his mind. It makes me wonder if Jesus ever shook His head sadly at Peter, wondering when or if he would grow and mature.

Thankfully for all of us, Peter did. Evidence of this is the fact that Peter was a leader in the early church (Galatians 2:9). He wrote two letters filled with words of wisdom. Three small words in his second letter caught my mind and my heart.

While you wait.

> *Waiting for Christ's return shouldn't be passive.*

While we wait for the new Heaven and earth that God promised (2 Peter 3:13-14 CSB). While we live here as foreigners and throughout our time as exiles. While we wait, there are things we can do. Waiting for Christ's return shouldn't be passive.

Peter tells us what to do while we are waiting. We should "grow in the grace and knowledge of our Lord and Savior Jesus Christ" (2 Peter 3:18).

What is this grace that Peter talks about? It is God's unmerited favor toward us. It's a gift we don't deserve. God gave it to us anyway, free of charge. It came at a substantial cost to Jesus, who died in our place, but costs us nothing.

Peter sets a wonderful example of someone who has grown in the grace of Jesus. He walked with Christ for three years. He ate meals with Jesus, witnessed His miracles, and listened to Him teach. Peter knew Jesus. Yet he denied Christ three times. Oh, Peter, why were you so fearful?

Can you imagine the grief that washed over Peter when he saw Jesus hanging from the cross? Think about the sorrow Peter felt when they took Jesus and placed Him in the tomb. He must have berated himself over and over for the denial of His Lord.

Now, think of the grace of Jesus, giving Peter something he didn't deserve. Three days later, we see this gift from Jesus to Peter.

Mary Magdalene stood at the tomb, looking for Jesus. But He wasn't there! Instead, an angel of the Lord was there and told Mary that Jesus has risen! "Go and tell His disciples **and Peter** that He will see you in Galilee" (Mark 16:7).

Jesus singled Peter out. He wanted Peter to know He forgave him. Jesus still considered Peter one of His disciples.[5] The grace of Jesus is so amazing!

While we wait, we can grow in grace and know Jesus more.

Growing in grace means continuously maturing as a Christian. We see this transformation in Peter. From an immature upstart to denying his Lord, to becoming a humble servant before Jesus (John 21:15-17). In John 21, Jesus asks Peter three times, "Do you love Me?"

Jesus was probably asking Peter, "Do you love Me more than these other disciples do?" After all, Peter had bragged about his love for

Christ and allegiance to Him (John 13:37, Matthew 26:33). Peter felt like his love of the Lord was greater than the other disciples.

So when Jesus asks about this love, we would expect Peter to boast again. Rather than becoming agitated and saying "Yes, I told You already, yes I absolutely love You more than these other guys." Instead, Peter simply says, "Yes, Lord, You know I do. You know all things (John 21:17, my paraphrase)." Peter yielded to Jesus, recognizing His sovereignty.

As Christians, we mature by knowing Jesus more and more. The scriptures teach us about Him. Our experiences with Him remind us He will never leave us. We pray to Him and trust Him.

We also learn from Peter that while we wait, we are to live "for the will of God" (1 Peter 4:2).

> *Exiles rejoice while they long for home.*

And what is God's will for us? Ah, the age-old question. And the Apostle Paul answers it. God's will for us is to rejoice always, pray without ceasing, and give thanks in everything (1 Thessalonians 5:16-18). Rejoice and praise Him for what He has done for us (saved us) and what He is doing in us (sanctifying us). Rejoice that we are God's chosen people, shining a bright light in a dark world. Exiles rejoice while they long for home.

While we wait, we pray constantly. For our homes, families, and friends. For our communities, cities, and states. We pray our nation will return to being a country that fears God, one nation under God. And we include the world in our prayers, praying for those who don't know Jesus and for those who know Jesus but face persecution because of it.

In everything, we give thanks, knowing that Jesus promises us a place in Heaven and a purpose here on earth.

Live with Anticipation and Expectation

As exiles, we rejoice and can't wait to get home. While we wait, we will wait with great anticipation and expectation.

But what's the difference?

Anticipation is looking forward to something with excitement or pleasure. It's when you feel eager about something that is going to happen. Anticipation carries great hope, as we are open to the possibilities about the future.

Expectation is looking forward to something with the belief or assumption that it will happen. You are positive something is going to happen. Expectation limits us to a specific outcome. If I don't pay my electric bill, I expect the power company to shut off my electricity.

The Hebrews in Egypt expected their exodus. One of their last meals in captivity was the Passover meal. It was a meal to commemorate their freedom from slavery. They were told to eat it in a hurry, ready to leave (Exodus 12:11). They dressed for travel, with their clothes on and sandals on their feet. Think of the excitement! The packed bags were ready and waiting by the door. There was a buzz of energy in the air. They were going home! I think they may have even slept with their shoes on. They were waiting for the call of the Lord.

Even the Ark was ready to go. The poles for carrying the Ark remained in the rings at all times (Exodus 25:14-15), attached to the side of the Ark. When God gave the word, the Hebrews lifted the Ark, and off they went!

The problem with expectations is they can leave us unfulfilled and discontent. Expectations presume a certain outcome. That's what happened to the Israelites after they left Egypt. It didn't take long for them to want to turn around and go back. Their expectations for travel were high. The Israelites assumed food and meat would be plentiful. After all, there was delicious meat in Egypt (Exodus 16:2-16). What they had was manna. God's food, but certainly not what they were used to.

In addition, when the scouts went into the Promised Land, they saw giants. These extra-large men scared the Israelites. They expected no opposition when they entered the promised land (Exodus 13:25-14:3). How could they possibly fight these enormous people?

When we rejoice as exiles, we live with excitement, anticipating our future home. We expect great things based on the truth of God's Word, not our preconceived notions. We have a steadfast hope while we wait. Our hope is a desire for something good and knowing we will obtain it (eternal life and living with Jesus). Our steadfastness is perseverance. We don't let circumstances and trials get us down or cause us to abandon hope.

Mingled with our great anticipation and confident expectation is joy.

God's grace brings joy to our lives. We have joy despite our circumstances. Happiness, on the other hand, depends on outside factors. Is the weather nice? Did my paycheck make it to the bank? Are my friends meeting me for lunch? Yes? Yay, we're happy. But when those outside factors don't turn out the way we'd like, our happiness crumbles. But joy? It exudes from us because of Christ in us. We choose joy because of God's presence and His promises. Because we hope in Christ, we will have joy that will last into eternity!

With supernatural joy, we live ready to meet Jesus.

Belong to Long

Rejoicing as exiles, we settle in where the Lord has placed us. We build homes and pray for the land of our captivity. While we wait, we live for God's will and grow in Christ. And we do not become comfortable!

Exiles anticipate their better home with joy and expect it will be just as God has promised us. If not better! It will be more than we could ask for or imagine.

Now what?

I have learned to be content with my longing. How? Because I realize I don't belong, I recognize Heaven is my home, and I rejoice that I am an exile for Christ. We are exiles on our way home wandering around in the wilderness a bit. For now, we belong here, longing for home. We stay homesick for our heavenly home.

And we don't get tired in the waiting.

One thing about Jesus and His time on earth is that He never grew weary of doing His Father's will. Jesus endured until the very end. We can live with endurance, too, when Christ Jesus empowers our lives.

We can persevere with patience until the end by looking at the lives of those who have gone before us. Hebrews 11 and 12 mention the heroes of the faith. These saints testify by their lives that they withstood hardship and adversity because of their faith. We look to their lives to cheer us on until the finish line.

I have a dear friend who forges ahead, blazing a trail in the writing world and technology. I look to her example and follow the path she cleared. She makes it easy for me to move forward. And she's one of my biggest cheerleaders.

The heroes of the faith are our great cloud of witnesses. Their lives encourage us. Along with Jesus, they have blazed the trail to the Father and toward home for us. The unknown is not nearly as fearful when someone goes before you to show you the way.

And if you happen to feel weary? Remember what Charles Spurgeon said: "By perseverance, the snail reached the ark."[6]

Journey Toward Home

God, with His faithful love, will lead the people He has redeemed. He will guide us to His holy dwelling with His strength (Exodus 15:13). Jesus' strength will guide us home.

> *Each day on earth is a step closer to our true home. Every step we take is a step closer to Jesus.*

Isn't that a comforting thought? Each day on earth is a step closer to our true home. Every step we take is a step closer to Jesus. His strength will hold us steady and bring us home to Him.

"When Jesus takes your hand, He keeps you tight. When Jesus keeps you tight, He leads you through your whole life. When Jesus leads you through your whole life, He brings you safely home."[7]

> *To live as an exile means to long for home. Don't lose the longing in your heart.*

To live as an exile is to long for home. When we set our hearts on pilgrimage, we know Jesus will bring us safely to His heavenly kingdom.

Until then, don't lose the longing in your heart. It's a reminder of where you truly belong.

• • • ● ● ● ● ● • • •

Stepping Stone #12

REJOICE:
You are an exile who longs to be home with Jesus.

REFLECT on God's Word:
Jeremiah 29:7
2 Peter 3:14

RESPOND to the questions:

- What are some things you find tempting to do "while you wait" for an event?

- What pulls you homeward? Keeps you homebound?

- Has there been a time when you've "grown weary" of doing good? How did you overcome those feelings?

READING TO ENJOY ON YOUR JOURNEY HOME

Alcorn, Randy. 2004. *Heaven*. Tyndale House Publishers.

Rhodes, Ron. 2009. *The Wonder of Heaven: A Biblical Tour of Our Eternal Home*. Harvest House Publishers.

Buchanan, Mark. 2002. *Things Unseen: Living in Light of Forever*. Multnomah Publishers, Inc.

Nina, Mabel. 2022. *Far From Home: Discovering Your Identity as Foreigners on Earth*. Iron Stream Harambee Press.

Guthrie, Nancy. 2018. *Even Better than Eden: Nine Ways the Bible's Story Changes Everything about Your Story*. Crossway.

Saunders, Caroline. 2024. *Come Home: Tracing God's Promise of Home through Scripture*. Lifeway.

Burpo, Todd. 2010. *Heaven Is for Real: A Little Boy's Astounding Story of His Trip to Heaven and Back*. Thomas Nelson.

Piper, Don. 2004. *90 Minutes in Heaven: A True Story of Death and Life*. Revell.

Jeffress, Dr. Robert. 2018. *A Place Called Heaven: 10 Surprising Truths about Your Eternal Home*. Baker Books

Eldredge, John. 2018. *All Things New: Heaven, Earth, and the Restoration of Everything You Love*. Thomas Nelson

Tada, Joni Eareckson. 2018. *Heaven: Your Real Home...From a Higher Perspective*. Zondervan.

Graham, Billy. 2012. *The Heaven Answer Book (Answer Book Series)*. Thomas Nelson.

SCRIPTURES TO PONDER ON YOUR JOURNEY HOME

Stranger:

- "I am a stranger and a sojourner among you; give me a burial site among you that I may bury my dead out of my sight." **Genesis 23:4**

- "Hear my prayer, O Lord, and give ear to my cry; Do not be silent at my tears; For I am a stranger with You, A sojourner like all my fathers." **Psalm 39:12**

- "I am a stranger in the earth; Do not hide Your commandments from me." **Psalm 119:19**

- "All these died in faith, without receiving the promises, but having seen them and having welcomed them from a distance, and having confessed that they were strangers and exiles on the earth." **Hebrews 11:13**

Identity:

- "Therefore if anyone is in Christ, *he is* a new creature; the old things passed away; behold, new things have come." **2 Corinthians 5:17**

- "But you are a chosen race, a royal priesthood, a holy nation, a people for God's own possession, so that you may proclaim the excellencies of Him who has called you out of darkness into His marvelous light" **1 Peter 2:9**

- "For we are His workmanship (masterpiece), created in Christ Jesus for good works, which God prepared beforehand so that we would walk in them." **Ephesians 2:10**

- "He who has an ear, let him hear what the Spirit says to the churches. To him who overcomes, to him I will give some of the hidden manna, and I will give him a white stone, and a new name written on the stone which no one knows but he who receives it." **Revelation 2:17**

Heaven:

- "For our citizenship is in heaven, from which also we eagerly wait for a Savior, the Lord Jesus Christ" **Philippians 3:20**

- "and He will wipe away every tear from their eyes; and there will no longer be any death; there will no longer be any mourning, or crying, or pain; the first things have passed away." **Revelation 21:4**

- "In My Father's house are many dwelling places; if it were not so, I would have told you; for I go to prepare a place for you." **John 14:2**

- "to obtain an inheritance which is imperishable and undefiled and will not fade away, reserved in heaven for you" **1 Peter 1:4**

Heavenly Mindset:

- "But store up for yourselves treasures in heaven, where neither moth nor rust destroys, and where thieves do not break in or steal; for where your treasure is, there your heart will be also." **Matthew 6:20–21**

- "So if you have been raised with the Messiah, seek what is above, where the Messiah is, seated at the right hand of God. Set your minds on what is above, not on what is on the earth." **Colossians 3:1–2**

- "Now, little children, abide in Him, so that when He appears, we may have confidence and not shrink away from Him in shame at His coming." **1 John 2:28**

- "Let the word of Christ richly dwell within you, with all wisdom teaching and admonishing one another with psalms *and* hymns *and* spiritual songs, singing with thankfulness in your hearts to God." **Colossians 3:16**

ACKNOWLEDGEMENTS

From my heart, thank you!

They say it takes a village. It definitely took that and more to get this book written. I could not have done it without the help and support of so many amazing people.

To my husband John, you have supported and encouraged me from the beginning of this long writing journey. You have given up day trips, loaded the dishwasher, and folded laundry more times than I can count so I could write. You listen to me as I work out kinks in the book. Most of all, you have prayed me through. Thank you. I love you.

To my brothers and sisters-in-law—Wayne and Tammy, Steve and Bebe—who walked with me through the loss of our Mama. Thank you. I love you more than you know.

A big hug to all the ladies in His Girls Gather, a writing and creative group: Thank you for letting me hang out with you. I have learned so much from all of you. We laughed and had a grand time along the way. I value your friendship!

Carmen Horne, my dear sweet friend! You always let me tell you, every year or so, that I would not, no never, write this book. You just smiled, nodded, and continued your prayers and encouragement. You believed in me and never gave up on me. You blazed the trail for me and shared all you learned. You are such a blessing.

Carmen, Kristine Brown, and Stephanie Adams. My goodness, what can I say? Thank you ladies for holding my hand and nursing me along. Thank you for listening to me whine and question myself. You read the book as I wrote it and offered valuable suggestions! Thank you for your time and your prayers!

To Dawn, Christi, Karen, and Susan, my beta readers. You gave up your valuable time to read the book. Thank you! But most of all, thank you for your hugs and prayers!

My church family. What a blessing it is to worship with you each Sunday. Y'all are the best group of encouragers. You are indeed the hands and feet of Jesus to so many, including me!

Liz Giertz, my editor. I'm so sorry for the punctuation and for-matting mess you had to wade through reading the manuscript. You taught me to love (almost) the Oxford comma, LOL! I appreciate all your insight.

Last, but certainly not least, to my Lord and Savior, Jesus Christ. Thank you for saving me, and preparing my dream home for me. I can't wait to see it! All glory to God the Father and God the Son for allowing me to write this book, and for never letting me give up. I pray it honors You and teaches others about the wonderful future we have with You!

ENDNOTES

Longing to Belong

1. My paraphrase of Genesis 12:13-16

2. Genesis 17:17 *Ellicott's Commentary for English Readers*, A Bible Commentary for English Readers by various writers. Edited by Charles John Ellicott. Cassell and Company, Ltd., London, Paris, New York & Melbourne, 1905, www.Biblehub.com accessed 8/22/22

3. Warren Baker and Eugene E. Carpenter, *The Complete Word Study Dictionary: Old Testament* (Chattanooga, TN: AMG Publishers, 2003), 212.

4. Warren Baker and Eugene E. Carpenter, *The Complete Word Study Dictionary: Old Testament* (Chattanooga, TN: AMG Publishers, 2003), 1221.

5. Edwin A. Blum, "John," in *The Bible Knowledge Commentary: An Exposition of the Scriptures*, ed. J. F. Walvoord and R. B. Zuck, vol. 2 (Wheaton, IL: Victor Books, 1985), 306.

Longing for Identity

1. Lotz, Anne Graham. *The Daniel Prayer* (p. 16). Zondervan. Kindle Edition.

2. Daniel 4:8, 5:13, 6:5, 13, 20

3. 1 These. 1:4, Colossians 3:12, Jude 1

4. "Historically, a white stone was given to victors at games for entrance to banquets (cf. the messianic banquet); such a stone was also used by jurors at trials to vote for acquittal." Crossway Bibles, The ESV Study Bible (Wheaton, IL: Crossway Bibles, 2008), 2466.

Longing for What Was

1. Lucado, Max. *God's Story, Your Story: When His Becomes Yours* (The Story) (p. 62). Zondervan. Kindle Edition.

2. The restoration temple (this present house), Haggai said, would have a glory greater than the Solomonic temple (the former house) because during Herodian times the presence of the Messiah would adorn it (cf. Matt. 12:6; John 2:13–22). (The Herodian temple was a continuation, in a sense, of the postexilic "second" temple, not a "third" temple.) F. Duane Lindsey, "Haggai," in *The Bible Knowledge Commentary: An Exposition of the Scriptures*, ed. J. F. Walvoord and R. B. Zuck, vol. 1 (Wheaton, IL: Victor Books, 1985), 1542.

3. "you yourselves, as living stones, a spiritual house, are being built to be a holy priesthood to offer spiritual sacrifices acceptable to God through Jesus Christ." Christian Standard Bible (Nashville, TN: Holman Bible Publishers, 2020), 1 Peter 2:5.

Longing for Home

1. analúō; fut. analúsō, to loose. Spiros Zodhiates, *The Complete Word Study Dictionary: New Testament* (Chattanooga, TN: AMG Publishers, 2000).

2. Galatians 1:12 (NLT) "I received my message from no human source, and no one taught me. Instead, I received it by direct revelation from Jesus Christ."

3. Alcorn, Randy. (2024, February 19). Facebook. [https://www.facebook.com/randyalcorn]

Why Learn About Heaven?

1. Wilkin, Jen. *Women of the Word: How to Study the Bible with Both Our Hearts and Our Minds* (p. 31). Crossway. Kindle Edition.

2. https://hymnary.org/text/o_soul_are_you_weary_and_troubled

3. Mark Twain, *The Adventures of Huckleberry Finn* (New York: Faucett Columbine, 1066), 6

4. Buchanan, Mark. *Things Unseen: Living in Light of Forever* (p. 76). The Crown Publishing Group. Kindle Edition.

5. Randy C. Alcorn, *Heaven* (Tyndale House Publishers, Inc., 2004), 412

6. Randy C. Alcorn, *Heaven* (Tyndale House Publishers, Inc., 2004), 411

7. 3857. παράδεισος parádeisos; gen. paradeísou, masc. noun. Paradise. This is an oriental word which the Greeks borrowed from the Persians, among whom it meant a garden, park Spiros Zodhiates, *The Complete Word Study Dictionary: New Testament* (Chattanooga, TN: AMG Publishers, 2000).

8. Alcorn, Randy. 2007. *Heaven.* Wheaton, IL: Tyndale House, page 42

9. https://www.epm.org/resources/2017/Apr/19/why-and-how-does-satan-lie-us-about-heaven/

Why Long for Heaven? I Like it Here!

1. https://www.epm.org/blog/2023/Sep/25/joy-imagining-heaven

2. Spiros Zodhiates, *The Complete Word Study Dictionary: New Testament* (Chattanooga, TN: AMG Publishers, 2000).

3. Ephesians 1:14; 2 Corinthians 5:5, 1:22

4. Spiros Zodhiates, *The Complete Word Study Dictionary: New Testament* (Chattanooga, TN: AMG Publishers, 2000)

5. James Strong, *Enhanced Strong's Lexicon* (Woodside Bible Fellowship, 1995).

6. Zodhiates, S. (2000). *The Complete Word Study Dictionary: New Testament* (electronic ed.). Chattanooga, TN: AMG Publishers.

7. Ibid

Why is Heaven Home and Whose Home Is It?

1. Spiros Zodhiates, *The Complete Word Study Dictionary: New Testament* (Chattanooga, TN: AMG Publishers, 2000).

2. Warren W. Wiersbe, *The Bible Exposition Commentary*, vol. 2 (Wheaton, IL: Victor Books, 1996), 91.

3. Warren W. Wiersbe, *The Bible Exposition Commentary*, vol. 1 (Wheaton, IL: Victor Books, 1996), 540

Why Do We Belong in Heaven?

1. Spiros Zodhiates, *The Complete Word Study Dictionary: New Testament* (Chattanooga, TN: AMG Publishers, 2000).

2. Warren W. Wiersbe, *The Bible Exposition Commentary*, vol. 2 (Wheaton, IL: Victor Books, 1996), 621

3. Wilkin, J. (2021). *Ten Words to Live By* (1st ed., p. 30). Crossway.

194

4. Crossway Bibles, The ESV Study Bible (Wheaton, IL: Crossway Bibles, 2008), 2423.

5. Warren W. Wiersbe, *The Bible Exposition Commentary*, vol. 2 (Wheaton, IL: Victor Books, 1996), 624.

6. Lewis, C.S. *Mere Christianity*. HarperCollins, 2001, p. 134

Rejoicing as Exiles

1. https://www.psychologytoday.com/us/blog/the-athletes-way/202204/creativity-flourishes-away-beaten-pathways-in-the-mind

2. Warren W. Wiersbe, *The Bible Exposition Commentary*, vol. 1 (Wheaton, IL: Victor Books, 1996), 27–28.

3. Charles Spurgeon (2011). *Strengthen My Spirit*, p.37, Barbour Publishing

4. Marshall, G. (2019). *The Promise of His Presence* (p. 25). P&R Publishing.

5. Louis A. Barbieri Jr., "Matthew," in *The Bible Knowledge Commentary: An Exposition of the Scriptures*, ed. J. F. Walvoord and R. B. Zuck, vol. 2 (Wheaton, IL: Victor Books, 1985), 33.

Rejoicing in Faith

1. Warren W. Wiersbe, *The Bible Exposition Commentary*, vol. 1 (Wheaton, IL: Victor Books, 1996), 695.

2. Mary DeMuth, *90 Day Bible Reading Challenge* (Minnesota: Bethany House Publishers, 2023), 169

3. Elisabeth Elliot. AZQuotes.com, Wind and Fly LTD, 2024. https://www.azquotes.com/author/17940-Elisabeth_Elliot, accessed May 03, 2024.

4. Warren W. Wiersbe, *The Bible Exposition Commentary*, vol. 1 (Wheaton, IL: Victor Books, 1996), 675.

Rejoicing in Confidence

1. 1 Peter 2:19, Philippians 1:29, 1 Thessalonians 3:4, 2 Timothy 1:8, 2 Timothy 3:12, John 15:20

2. *thaumastós*; fem. *thaumasté*, neut. *thaumastón*, adj. from *thaumázō* (2296), to marvel. Wonderful, admirable, wondrous. Spiros Zodhiates, *The Complete Word Study Dictionary: New Testament,* (Chattanooga, TN: AMG Publishers, 2000).

3. Marshall, Glenna. *Memorizing Scripture: The Basics, Blessings, and Benefits of Meditating on God's Word* (pp. 100-102). Moody Publishers. Kindle Edition

4. J. Ronald Blue, "James," in *The Bible Knowledge Commentary: An Exposition of the Scriptures*, ed. J. F. Walvoord and R. B. Zuck, vol. 2 (Wheaton, IL: Victor Books, 1985), 821.

5. Horne, Carmen. *Grace Maps: Our Journey Guided by God's Grace.* Cotton Port Publishing, LLC, 2022. pp. 23, 43-44

6. Susie Larson used this phrase at a women's conference.

Rejoicing While You Long for Home

1. Elisabeth Elliot. AZQuotes.com, Wind and Fly LTD, 2024. https://www.azquotes.com/quote/712404, accessed May 03, 2024.

2. Warren W. Wiersbe, *The Bible Exposition Commentary*, vol. 2 (Wheaton, IL: Victor Books, 1996), 158.

3. Marshall, Glenna. *Memorizing Scripture: The Basics, Blessings, and Benefits of Meditating on God's Word* (p. 111). Moody Publishers. Kindle Edition.

4. Warren W. Wiersbe, *The Bible Exposition Commentary*, vol. 1 (Wheaton, IL: Victor Books, 1996), 367–368.

5. John D. Grassmick, "Mark," in *The Bible Knowledge Commentary: An Exposition of the Scriptures*, ed. J. F. Walvoord and R. B. Zuck, vol. 2 (Wheaton, IL: Victor Books, 1985), 193.

6. *"The Salt-cellars: Being a Collection of Proverbs, Together with Homely Notes Thereon"* by Charles Spurgeon, (p. 89), 1889.

7. Corrie ten Boom, *In My Father's House* (Eureka, MT:Lighthouse Trails Publishing, 2011), 146

ABOUT THE AUTHOR

Ellen pens her stories from the Bayou Country of South Louisiana, where gumbo and crawfish reign and majestic oaks shade weary sojourners. When not writing and mining the depths of God's Word, you can find Ellen digging in her flower beds, relaxing on the back porch, or traveling with her husband John. She and John have four awesome grandkids.

Ellen has loved writing since high school, but this passion lay dormant for many decades. When her mom passed away in 2011,

Ellen felt the Lord urging her to put pen to paper and write. She shares deep truths from God's Word in teachable, relatable, and often funny tales that help women see God's faithfulness in their lives.

Passionate about scripture, Ellen desires to see others dig into God's Word and thirst after Him with all their hearts. A detective at heart, Ellen shares her scriptural discoveries on her blog, encouraging her readers to soak in God's Word and sprout seeds of faith.

Ellen has contributed to Deeper Waters, Word Nerd Wednesday, The Laundry Moms, Sweet to the Soul Faith Magazine, and Sweet to the Soul Ministries. She has also written for *The Message*, a study magazine published annually by the women's department of WE-GOM, a nondenominational evangelistic organization in Nigeria.

To connect with Ellen, visit her online at *EllenChauvin.com*.

CONNECT WITH ELLEN

Soaked & Sprouting

Ellen Chauvin

Soaked in God's Word, Sprouting Seeds of Faith

www.EllenChauvin.com

www.ingramcontent.com/pod-product-compliance
Lightning Source LLC
LaVergne TN
LVHW051049080426
835508LV00019B/1785